BETWEEN
YOU AND

AI

BETWEEN YOU AND

Unlock the **Power of Human Skills**
to Thrive in an AI-Driven World

ANDREA IORIO

WILEY

Published by John Wiley & Sons, Inc., Hoboken, New Jersey.
Published simultaneously in Canada.

For general information on our other products and services or for technical support, please contact our Customer Care Department within the United States at (800) 762-2974, outside the United States at (317) 572-3993 or fax (317) 572-4002.

Wiley also publishes its books in a variety of electronic formats. Some content that appears in print may not be available in electronic formats. For more information about Wiley products, visit our web site at www.wiley.com.

Library of Congress Cataloging-in-Publication Data is Available:

ISBN: 9781394357987 (Cloth)
ISBN: 9781394357994 (ePub)
ISBN: 9781394358007 (ePDF)

Cover Design: Jon Boylan
Cover Images: © piai/stock.adobe.com;
            © Accountanz/stock.adobe.com

SKY10127614_100625

Contents

Introduction

IN THE 1800s, during the Golden Age of gold mining and railroad expansion in the United States, there lived a man that, according to folklore, was considered the strongest alive. His name was John Henry—a steel driver who shattered massive rock with unmatched power, carving tunnels through mountains with his sledgehammer. Day after day, with sheer strength and unwavering resolve, John Henry struck each blow with the force of a lifetime of toil and pride. No other human could outdo him.

But the major threat to his dominance did not come from fellow workers in flesh and bone, but from ones in steel. Technological progress was relentless indeed. One fateful day, a salesperson arrived at John Henry's construction site, unveiling a mechanical marvel—a steam-powered drilling machine that he claimed would outwork any human laborer.

To John Henry, this was more than just a sales pitch; it was a direct challenge to his very identity. Unwilling to accept that any machine could surpass human strength and skill, he proposed a contest: he challenged the salesperson to determine who—him or the machine—could drill the deepest hole in a single day.

Confident in the power of his invention, the salesperson agreed. At dawn, the contest began. The machine roared to life, its piston hammering away with relentless precision, while beside it, John Henry swung his sledgehammer with determination, but at nowhere near the same speed. Although he was already lagging behind, his fellow workers cheered, their voices blending with the rhythmic clang of metal against stone.

Hour after hour, the machine surged ahead, its endurance seemingly limitless, drilling a 9-foot hole into the rock—far ahead of John Henry. But just when the outcome seemed inevitable, the unexpected happened: due to a mechanical dysfunction, the machine broke down under the strain.

John Henry, undeterred, pressed on. His blows grew heavier, his determination fiercer. By the end of the day, he eventually not only caught up to the stuck machine but surpassed it, winning the contest by digging an impressive 14-foot hole. He had outperformed the steam-powered drill, proving that human strength and resilience could triumph over mechanical innovation.

Yet victory came at a cost. As the dust settled and cheers filled the air, an exhausted John Henry collapsed at the foot of the mountain, his hammer still clutched in his hand. His heart, pushed beyond its limits, gave out just moments after his triumph.

Though he had won the battle, he had paid the ultimate price with his life.

Although the legend of John Henry exists in many versions, they all share the same bittersweet lesson: the story of a man who refused to be replaced by a machine, believing that human strength and spirit could never be outdone by technology. It is a tale of defiance and of humanity's innate resistance when faced with threats to its dominance.

But the true purpose of this tale is to make us wonder: What if John Henry had survived?

Surely, months later, the salesperson would have returned with an improved machine—stronger, faster, designed to overcome the mechanical shortcomings that caused it to break. Sort of a drilling machine 2.0.

John Henry, true to his spirit, would have challenged it once more—perhaps even won again. But for how long could that cycle continue? With each return, the machine would come back better—improved not by itself, but by the hands and minds of its inventors, who would learn from each failure, tweak its design, and increase its power. Eventually, the inevitable day would come when even John Henry's legendary strength would not be enough. At that point, he would have to face a choice: keep fighting an unwinnable battle or adapt to a new reality—one where technology had outperformed him at the very physical skill that defined him.

Today, as Artificial Intelligence (AI) accelerates at an ever-increasing pace and permeates every aspect of our life and work with its power, we are confronted with a question that is more pressing than ever: How can humans thrive in an era where AI is automating not just manual labor, but thinking itself? Unlike John Henry's mechanical rival, AI is a tool that thinks, learns, and evolves at an accelerating pace, mimicking and outperforming humans in a much broader range of skills than at any other point in time—and this time not only coming for our muscles, but for our brains. Like John Henry, we must decide: Do we resist, or do we evolve?

This dilemma is not unique to AI. It is a recurring theme in history. Time and again, humans have had to redefine their value when confronted with new technology that is capable of performing our tasks better than we can. The Industrial Revolution, factory automation, and now AI—each has challenged the existing hierarchy of skills. But to truly understand how we got to this point, we must look further back—to the very origins of human survival and the skills that originally determined success.

From Physical to Cognitive Skills

Deep in the remote southwestern corner of Ethiopia, nestled within the Omo Valley, lives the Suri tribe—an indigenous community known for their striking body decorations, including intricate scarification and iconic lip plates, as well as their deeply traditional way of life. The Suri are seminomadic cattle herders who primarily cultivate sorghum, and their access to modern technology is nearly nonexistent. Ironically, the most advanced tools at their disposal are weapons smuggled from nearby South Sudan, used to defend their livestock from rival tribes seeking to steal their cattle.

Another weapon in their hands—though far more rudimentary—is the *Bire*, a wooden stick that plays a crucial role in their traditional *Donga* ceremony. This event serves as a rite of passage, marking a Suri boy's transition from adolescence to manhood, proving his strength and readiness to care for a family. The initiation unfolds through an intense, often brutal fight, where opponents strike each other with powerful blows from the *Bire*. Picture these young boys as gladiators in an arena of people—the entire tribe encircles them, watching intently to see who will emerge as the proudest and strongest warrior. The winner of the *Donga* ceremony earns not only status but also the right to choose his desired partner. By winning the fight, he secures greater reproductive opportunities and solidifies his place within the tribe, ensuring his success in Suri society.

The correlation between physical attributes and better life outcomes has been a recurring pattern throughout human history. Between 130,000 and 80,000 years ago, the world saw the emergence of modern *Homo sapiens*, who originated in Africa and organized into small, tightly knit tribes of hunters and gatherers. They led highly mobile, nomadic lives, constantly moving to track food sources and adapt to shifting environmental conditions. Their survival depended on the ability to hunt game using spears and other primitive weapons crafted from stone—a cutting-edge technology for their time and a crucial lifeline for existence. Alongside hunting, they foraged for fruits, nuts, and edible plants, sustaining themselves on whatever the land provided.

In those days, the rules of survival were brutally simple. Strength and endurance reigned supreme. The most formidable warriors could chase prey for miles, wielding weapons with the precision and force needed to bring down animals far larger than themselves. A tribe's dominance—its ability to protect its people and secure sustenance—often depended on its strongest and most resilient members. Physical prowess wasn't just an asset; it was a lifeline. Those who were faster, stronger, and more robust earned their place at the forefront of tribal life, ensuring their survival in an unforgiving world.

Of course, cognitive skills and adaptability also played a role, but they were far less of a differentiator than physical abilities. In a world with limited access to external information and an oral, rather than written, tradition, people's cognitive abilities were largely uniform. Without exposure to new ideas, diverse knowledge, or complex problem-solving beyond their immediate environment, intelligence was constrained by the shared experiences of the tribe.

In a world where cognitive skills were undifferentiated, the real competitive advantage lay in physical prowess. Greater endurance meant a higher success rate in hunting, while superior strength made carving weapons from stone more efficient. In this harsh reality, those who excelled physically had the greatest chances of survival and success.

This skills paradigm—what we might call *physical leadership*— began to shift over time. From around 11,000 BCE, with the emergence of the first agricultural settlements, throughout the Industrial Revolution, and up until today, new technologies gradually leveled the physical playing field. Innovations such the plow, steam engines, and electricity provided broader access to physical power, often surpassing human capabilities and making raw physical strength less of a scarce advantage.

As these technologies advanced, they gave rise to a new skills paradigm—one we can call *cognitive leadership*. After all, if a single steam engine could lift, press, and transport with a force no human could match, the fundamental question shifted. If machines could now perform the tasks that once defined the strongest *Homo sapiens* (as illustrated by the John Henry story) and access to these machines became widespread, what skills would become the most valuable in life and work? The answer, once again, lies in the concept of skills scarcity—this time not in muscles but in brains. Individuals would rise to success by mastering knowledge and cognitive skills that were rare and difficult to acquire. Think of technical expertise such as engineering, law, and medicine, which required years of education and training, or of cognitive abilities such as data analysis or logical thinking, which were not universally accessible.

Spoiler alert: Today, we stand at another turning point. The dominance of cognitive skills is now being disrupted by AI, forcing us to rethink what it means to lead and succeed in an era where machines can match or surpass many of our mental abilities.

In this book, I argue that we must embrace a new skills paradigm—*hybrid leadership*—that integrates both the AI literacy skills and the uniquely human skills that are now necessary to thrive at work and in life.

It is important to keep in mind that skills tend to determine a person's success in life and the workplace precisely when they are scarce—namely, when most others either don't possess them, don't reach the same level of proficiency, or don't have the same access to acquiring them—and, of course, when they are high in demand. Take lawyers, for example. If you've ever needed one, you know their services come at a hefty price, and this is because few people are willing to endure the years of rigorous study and training required to master the law. Their specialized knowledge is rare, and rarity commands value. Now, imagine a hypothetical city where, by some coincidence, every resident chose to study law and acquired the same level of expertise. Would lawyers still be able to charge high fees? Of course not. The economist in me can't help but draw a parallel to supply and demand: When there is an oversupply of a skill, its value diminishes—just as it would if Hermès suddenly mass-produced Birkin bags, making them widely available.

As a result of mechanical innovations, cognitive abilities—not physical strength—became the currency of success. In that new reality, the workforce began to split into two distinct groups: those with superior cognitive skills and those without.

Those with superior cognitive skills, capable of understanding and leveraging these powerful technological tools, ascended to positions of influence and leadership. Engineers, inventors, and industrialists stood at the helm, driving progress and reaping the rewards of innovation. Those who lacked these capabilities found themselves operating the very machines that defined the Industrial Age, confined to repetitive tasks dictated by the demands of the new economy.

It was no longer enough to endure or overpower. Success depended on cognitive abilities—such as the capacity to absorb and retain knowledge, think logically, and be creative. Those who could adapt their minds, not just their bodies, thrived in an increasingly mechanized world.

But then, everything changed again. The world went digital.

From Cognitive to Hybrid Skills

The cognitive skills paradigm, which has dominated for centuries, is now under immense pressure. If cognitive skills were the last frontier of human dominance, what happens when AI begins to erode that advantage? Few statements capture this shift more powerfully than the words of NVIDIA's CEO, Jensen Huang:

"Children shouldn't learn to write code."[1]

Would you ever expect such a statement from the CEO of one of the world's leading tech companies?

Huang made this counterintuitive statement at the World Government Summit in Dubai. He argued that even at this early stage of the AI revolution, writing code is no longer an essential skill. This seems paradoxical in a world where, according to the World Economic Forum's *Future of Jobs Report 2025*,[2] technology-related roles are projected to be the fastest-growing jobs between 2025 and 2030. These jobs include big data specialists, fintech engineers, AI and machine learning specialists, and—yes—software and application developers.

Yet Huang stood firm in his stance: "It's our job to create computational technology in such a way that no one needs to program," he told Summit attendees. "Everyone in the world is now a programmer. This is the miracle of Artificial Intelligence."

Indeed, thanks to AI, anyone can now be a programmer. With generative AI tools like OpenAI's Codex or GitHub Copilot, even someone with no technical background can generate functional code simply by asking the right question—or, as we'll explore later, crafting the right prompt. But it doesn't stop there. Today, AI enables anyone to be a translator, a copywriter, a filmmaker, a doctor, a designer—the list goes on. The possibilities are virtually endless.

If you work in any of these fields, you might find this assertion irritating—but that's likely because you're still holding on to traditional definitions of work. It's true: If we define a programmer's role primarily as writing lines of code, then yes, anyone can now be a programmer. The skill of writing code is no longer scarce; access to it has been democratized through Generative AI tools.

However, if we agree—as this book sets out to argue—that being a programmer in the age of AI requires a new set of skills, the picture changes. Skills such as reviewing code, understanding its broader implications, prompting AI tools efficiently, and thinking strategically about the architecture of a digital product become far more critical. In this sense, AI doesn't replace programmers; it enhances them. It augments their human work. With AI handling much of the coding itself, developers are no longer just code writers. They might become systems thinkers, product architects, and strategic collaborators that can focus on higher-level tasks. I say *might* because this potential depends entirely on their ability to develop these newly essential skills.

We're already seeing this shift in the real world. During Google's 2024 third quarter earnings call, CEO Sundar Pichai revealed that AI systems now generate over 25% of the new code for Google's products,[3] with human programmers overseeing and refining these AI-generated contributions. And Google isn't alone. Developers across the industry are embracing AI-assisted coding. According to Stack Overflow's 2024 survey,[4] 76% of respondents are either already using AI coding tools or planning to integrate them into their workflow.

AI's coding capabilities are also advancing rapidly. In a conversation on *The Joe Rogan Experience* podcast, Meta CEO Mark Zuckerberg stated, "Meta, as well as other companies, will have an AI that can effectively be a mid-level engineer at your company, capable of writing code."[5]

This rapid integration of AI into technical fields like coding is just the beginning. Just as the steam drill reshaped John Henry's world, AI is transforming the modern workplace, not only redefining the limits of what machines can accomplish but also expanding the possibilities of what humans can achieve.

The reality is that the skills required in the workplace are already evolving, and employers are taking notice. According to the World Economic Forum's *Future of Jobs Report 2025*, an estimated 39% of current workforce skills will be transformed or rendered obsolete between 2025 and 2030. This shift is also reflected in a survey my company conducted for this book, entitled "AI's Impact on Human Skills in the Workplace." We surveyed 217 global executives and found that already more than 41% of executives believe that more than one-fourth of their daily tasks can be automated, while 53% of them report that AI makes the quality of their work "better" or "much better."

AI's impact on the workplace is profound, as human workers increasingly collaborate with AI in ways that can feel both empowering and unsettling. On the one hand, AI acts as a powerful assistant—enhancing productivity, streamlining workflows, and amplifying human capabilities. On the other, it can feel like a direct competitor—executing tasks faster, with greater efficiency, fewer errors, continuous learning, and no fatigue—raising legitimate concerns about job displacement.

This dual dynamic—AI as both a collaborator and a competitor—is reshaping the nature of work, compelling professionals to reassess their roles, acquire new skills, and adapt to a future where Human Intelligence and AI must not only coexist, but actively complement one another.

Friend or Foe: The Challenges of Collaborating with AI

Turning AI into a true collaborator rather than a competitor is no simple task. Many organizations struggle to integrate AI effectively—not due to limitations in the technology itself, but because successful adoption requires more than just implementation. It demands a fundamental shift in mindset, skills, and organizational culture.

The challenge often begins with AI literacy. Employees and leaders alike may lack the knowledge to fully harness AI's potential, resulting in inefficient use or failure to integrate AI into workflows in a way that genuinely enhances productivity. In other cases, AI adoption is stalled by organizational inertia, as companies remain entrenched in legacy systems and processes, resisting the transformative changes AI demands. Additionally, fear and skepticism play a significant role—many professionals worry that embracing AI could ultimately make their roles obsolete, leading to hesitation and resistance rather than a proactive approach to collaboration.

Whether AI will become our greatest collaborator or our fiercest competitor will depend largely on us. Two key factors will determine this outcome: first, how effectively we learn to leverage AI tools to enhance productivity and efficiency and second, how well we adapt our skills to complement, rather than compete with, these rapidly evolving technologies.

Why This Book—And Why Now?

The purpose of this book is to address one of the most pressing questions facing professionals, leaders, and organizations today: What skills are essential, not just to avoid being replaced, but to truly thrive in the age of AI?

Just as John Henry faced an existential crossroads, so do we. The difference? This time, we don't have to collapse from exhaustion trying to beat the machines. Instead, we can choose a different path—one that amplifies what makes us uniquely human and unlocks AI's potential as our greatest collaborator.

John Henry's story is a powerful reminder that technology, no matter how advanced, remains a tool. The real transformation lies in the skills we choose to develop, prioritize, and refine as we navigate an era of rapid technological change.

I personally felt a strong urge to write this book because in my work as a keynote speaker engaging with over 100 companies each year—including many Fortune 500 firms—I've noticed a recurring challenge. It's not the technology itself that creates the biggest hurdle, but the human transformation required to ensure people stay not just relevant, but even more valuable in the age of AI.

Was This Book Written by AI?

Since this is a book about AI, let's address a question that may come to mind right away: Was this book written by AI? The answer is no—this book was written by a human (myself, a human, despite the irony that my initials are also AI). However, it was written by a human who leveraged AI at various stages of the process to enhance both efficiency and quality.

Two AI tools, in particular, have been my companions throughout this journey. ChatGPT served as my proofreader, helping to refine my writing and correct mistakes (an invaluable aid, given that writing a book in English isn't always intuitive for a native Italian speaker). Meanwhile, Perplexity.ai acted as my research assistant, helping me find relevant references and supporting materials.

Rather than replacing my role as an author, AI augmented my capabilities as an author—just as much as it is reshaping countless professions today. I should also note that the final output has been refined by "human" developmental editors and proofreaders, reinforcing a key idea that will be emphasized throughout this book—that the AI–human partnership is, in most cases, the best possible scenario.

Chapter by Chapter: What to Expect from the Book

The book is structured as follows: Chapter 1 takes a close look at where we currently stand—both in terms of what AI can do and how human skills compare. It also lays the groundwork for a concept that appears throughout the book: the "hybrid skillset," a model that outlines the key human abilities we must prioritize in order to thrive in the age of AI.

From there, the book is divided into three sections:

- Section I: Cognitive Transformation
- Section II: Behavioral Transformation
- Section III: Emotional Transformation

Each section explores a distinct dimension of human adaptation, outlining the key competencies needed not only to remain relevant but to thrive in a world increasingly shaped by AI.

Section I comprises Chapters 2, 3, and 4, each focusing on a critical cognitive skill essential for thriving in an AI-driven world:

- Chapter 2: Prompting—The ability to ask better questions, both to AI systems and to humans, in order to extract more relevant, insightful, and actionable information
- Chapter 3: Data Sensemaking—The ability to interpret, contextualize, and derive meaning from AI-generated inputs and outputs, ensuring informed and strategic decision-making
- Chapter 4: Reperception—The ability to update decisions, beliefs, and ideas in response to external change, fostering creativity and continuous learning

Section II comprises Chapters 5, 6, and 7, each focusing on a key behavioral skill necessary for navigating an AI-driven world:

- Chapter 5: Augmentation—The ability to automate routine tasks while strategically using the time saved to augment—to enhance and elevate—the quality of human work
- Chapter 6: Adaptability—The ability to respond to external change, innovating and experimenting in an era of uncertainty and transformation
- Chapter 7: Antifragility—The ability to maximize learning from mistakes while minimizing their cost, fostering a culture of continuous improvement and innovation

Section III comprises Chapters 8, 9, and 10, each focusing on a critical emotional skill necessary for thriving in an AI-driven world:

- Chapter 8: Empathy—The ability to connect with others by understanding and sharing their emotions, fostering deeper relationships and meaningful human interactions
- Chapter 9: Trust—The ability to collaborate effectively by embracing vulnerability and reciprocation, strengthening both human-to-human and human-to-AI partnerships
- Chapter 10: Agency—The ability to take responsibility not only for our actions but also for outcomes beyond our direct control, ensuring ethical and informed execution in collaboration with AI

The Conclusion ties together the book's main concepts, reinforcing the essential skills needed to thrive in the age of AI while laying out a path forward for continued growth and adaptation. It serves as both a reflection on the transformation explored throughout the chapters and a call to action for embracing the AI–human partnership with confidence and purpose.

Welcome to this transformative journey, and . . . *buona fortuna!*

1

Understanding Artificial Intelligence

In the early hours of 8 October 2024, a man lay sleeping in a cheap California motel room. He had taken the next day off from his job as an AI researcher and university professor to undergo an MRI at a nearby hospital.

At about 2:00 a.m., his phone rang, abruptly pulling him from a deep sleep. Half-conscious, he instinctively reached for his phone and answered in a groggy voice. On the other end of the line, a calm but firm voice spoke after confirming his identity: "Dr. Hinton, we are calling to inform you that you have been awarded the 2024 Nobel Prize in Physics."

For a brief moment, he wasn't sure if he was dreaming.

Perhaps it was some cruel prank or a misdialed number. Nobel Prizes aren't exactly announced in the middle of the night, and, at that moment, he certainly didn't feel like someone who had just joined the ranks of history's most celebrated scientists. After all, his research was in AI, not in physics. Still half asleep, he squinted at his phone's screen and noticed the caller ID indicated a Swedish number. He thought, "Wait a minute. . . . The Nobel Prize committee is based in Sweden. Could this actually be real?" The unmistakable Swedish accent of the caller was a detail that lent credibility to the surreal moment, but he hesitated further. He knew well that AI-generated voices could mimic foreign accents, as AI was precisely the kind of technology he had spent his entire career researching and developing. But as he listened

1

more closely, he realized multiple people—all with the same distinct Scandinavian intonation—were on the line. That's when it hit him: this was real. He—Geoffrey Hinton, professor at the University of Toronto, often hailed as the godfather of AI—had just won the 2024 Nobel Prize in Physics, which was jointly granted to John J. Hopfield of Princeton University. The award came as a surprise given that AI is not traditionally linked to physics. But as the reality sank in, it became clear that this was a historic recognition of Hinton's and Hopfield's pioneering work from the 1980s on neural networks, which are the foundation of modern AI and draw inspiration from the laws of physics. Once dismissed as abstract theory, their work now underpins some of the most powerful AI systems of the twenty-first century, driving everything from Large Language Models (LLMs)—AI systems trained on vast amounts of text to understand and generate humanlike language—to groundbreaking scientific discoveries.

In fact, neural networks led to yet another significant AI milestone at the 2024 Nobel Prizes—in Chemistry. The award recognized a trio of scientists who harnessed machine learning to predict protein structures, a breakthrough with far-reaching implications for medicine and biotechnology. Among the recipients were Demis Hassabis, co-founder of DeepMind (acquired by Google in 2014), and his colleague John Jumper. Their groundbreaking AI model, AlphaFold, solved a decades-old biological mystery, accurately predicting the intricate 3D structures of proteins from their amino acid sequences—a challenge that had long defied conventional scientific methods.

The excitement surrounding the awarding of Nobel Prizes has always been about more than just accolades; the prizes can be seen as a reflection of the collective *zeitgeist*, capturing the defining conversations of each era, and in 2024, that conversation was unmistakably about AI.

But how did we get here? After all, for decades, Artificial Intelligence was more of a theoretical dream than a reality. In the 1940s, Alan Turing laid the groundwork, envisioning machines that could simulate human reasoning, and the field officially took shape in 1956, when John McCarthy introduced the term *Artificial Intelligence* at the Dartmouth Conference, sparking waves of optimism. But progress wasn't linear. AI went through cycles of hype and disillusionment—so-called "AI winters"—when early systems failed to meet expectations, leading to funding cuts and skepticism.

Today, however, as evidenced by the recipients of the 2024 Nobel Prizes in both Physics and Chemistry, optimism has replaced skepticism. AI has reached an unprecedented level of maturity, moving from theoretical promise to real-world impact.

What Exactly Is AI?

Although *AI* is a term that today dominates headlines, boardroom discussions, and even casual conversations, its true meaning remains widely misunderstood. At its core, *Artificial Intelligence* refers to the ability of computational systems to perform tasks traditionally associated with human intelligence—such as learning, reasoning, problem-solving, perception, decision-making, and even recognizing emotions.

AI functions by processing vast datasets through sophisticated algorithms, allowing it to identify patterns, draw insights, and improve their performance over time. But unlike traditional software, which follows rigid, pre-programmed instructions, AI systems can adapt dynamically, refining their outputs based on new information and past experiences. This ability to learn and evolve is what makes AI not just a tool, but a transformative force shaping industries, innovation, and the future of work.

Data, Hardware, and Algorithms

A convergence of key factors has enabled AI to evolve and integrate seamlessly into both daily life and the workplace. At the heart of this progress lies a powerful triad: hardware, data, and algorithms.

- *Hardware* provides the physical infrastructure, or computing power, for AI. Specialized processors like GPUs (Graphics Processing Units) and TPUs (Tensor Processing Units)—designed specifically to handle large-scale mathematical operations—have dramatically accelerated model training by enabling massive parallel computations. The hardware allows today's complex models to be trained in days instead of years.

- *Data* is the fuel AI depends on to learn. Thanks to the Internet of Things (IoT)—a vast network of connected devices like sensors, wearables, and even home assistants—we now generate unprecedented amounts of data every second. Cloud computing, which refers to the delivery of computing services (like storage, processing, and software) over the internet, helps store and scale this data efficiently across distributed systems.
- *Algorithms* are the engines designed to recognize patterns, make predictions, and generate outputs from data. Among the most important are the neural networks—algorithms inspired by the structure of the human brain, composed of layers of interconnected nodes (or "neurons") that process information and learn from data through training. Neural networks form the foundation of deep learning, which is a subset of machine learning— the branch of AI focused on building systems that improve their performance over time by learning from data, without being explicitly programmed.

It's the convergence and maturation of these three elements— hardware, data, and algorithms—that has made AI not only viable, but widely adopted across industries, transforming how we work, make decisions, and live our daily lives.

Narrow AI and General AI

When thinking about the role of AI in the world today, there are two types of AI that we should consider: Narrow AI and General AI.

The AI tools we interact with daily—especially in the workplace— fall under the category of *Narrow AI*. These systems are designed to perform specific tasks with remarkable efficiency, whether it is recommending products, optimizing logistics, detecting fraud, or automating customer service. However, despite their advanced capabilities, they operate within strictly defined parameters and lack the broad adaptability, reasoning, and self-awareness of human intelligence. They can analyze, predict, and generate content, but they do so within the confines of its training data. You can think of Narrow AI as a hyperspe-cialized expert.

But Narrow AI is just the beginning. Progress in AI development is now bringing us closer to the next frontier: *General AI*, or *Artificial General Intelligence* (AGI). Unlike Narrow AI, which is limited to spe-cific tasks, AGI would possess the ability to reason, learn, and adapt across a broad range of fields and activities, much like a human. It would also think abstractly and make decisions with a level of flexibil-ity and independence that no AI system has yet achieved.

Think of AGI as a true generalist thinker. Its arrival would mark a profound shift—moving AI from a set of powerful but specialized tools to machines capable of true cognitive flexibility, problem-solving across disciplines, and even self-directed learning. While AGI remains a theoretical goal, the rapid pace of AI development suggests that its arrival is a question of *when*, rather than *if*.

AI's Impact in the Real World

Throughout history, technology has continuously reshaped the way we worked: the steam engine mechanized labor, electricity powered facto-ries, and the internet digitized communication and commerce. Like AI, these innovations are classified as *General Purpose Technologies* (GPTs)—foundational advancements that drive widespread economic and societal transformation and that share three key characteristics: (1) they have broad applications across all industries, (2) they con-tinuously evolve and improve over time, and (3) they spur the devel-opment of other innovations.

These developments aren't just incremental—they are revolution-ary. For the first time, we have a technology that doesn't just automate tasks, but amplifies human potential, unlocking productivity, creativ-ity, and insights at a scale never before imagined. From streamlining workflows to generating new ideas, AI is quickly becoming a co-pilot for professionals across nearly every industry: it enables smarter deci-sions, faster execution, and more personalized experiences. In that sense, AI isn't just reshaping work—it's reimagining what humans are capable of achieving.

What was once confined to research labs and to the minds of academics such as Geoffrey Hinton and John Hopfield is now embedded in the very fabric of how businesses operate, make decisions, and compete in an increasingly AI-driven landscape. Consequently, AI is enabling companies of all sizes—whether long-established industry leaders or agile startups—to reinvent their business models, optimize processes, and enhance their tools with a clear end goal: to deliver greater value to customers and drive accelerated growth.

Several forward-thinking companies are already leveraging AI to stay ahead of the curve:

- Agricultural machinery leader John Deere is integrating AI-powered automation and computer vision into its farming equipment, enabling precision agriculture and maximizing crop yields.
- Consumer goods giant Unilever is harnessing AI-driven analytics to optimize its supply chain, predict consumer trends, and develop hyper-personalized marketing strategies.
- The world's most valuable carmaker Tesla continues to push the boundaries of AI with its self-driving technology, using machine learning to improve vehicle autonomy and manufacturing efficiency.
- Engineering powerhouse Siemens is embedding AI into its "smart factories," enhancing predictive maintenance, increasing operational efficiency, and reducing energy consumption.
- Music industry disruptor Spotify is revolutionizing music discovery by employing AI-driven recommendation engines to curate personalized playlists and enhance user engagement.

The Risks of AI

AI is no silver bullet, and it does not come without risks. While some tech enthusiasts are eager to embrace AI's potential, most people remain deeply concerned. Worries range from ethical dilemmas and AI turning against humanity to job displacement and the risks of AI hallucinations (when AI generates information that sounds plausible but is entirely false or fabricated)—and not without reason.

For decades, Hollywood has reflected these fears, often portraying AI as a malevolent force. Think of the Replicants in *Blade Runner*, humanoid robots that rebel against their creators, or Skynet in *The Terminator*, an autonomous superintelligence that triggers a nuclear apocalypse to eradicate humanity. These anxieties have even extended beyond fiction, prompting a group of AI experts and tech executives to issue an open letter calling for a pause in the development of AI systems more powerful than Open AI's GPT-4, one of the most advanced language models available, known for its ability to generate human-like text, write code, and perform complex reasoning tasks. Their plea, however, went unanswered.

But when we zoom into AI's specific impact on the human skill set, three key risks emerge: (1) the risk of substitution, (2) the risk of dependence, and (3) the risk of commoditization.

Risk of Substitution

The first risk is substitution—the fear that AI will replace so many of our skills that humans themselves become redundant. A report by investment bank Goldman Sachs[1] warned that AI could displace the equivalent of 300 million full-time jobs and automate a quarter of all work tasks in the United States and Europe over the next decade. These numbers scream "substitution," fueling concerns that AI's rapid advancements may one day render many human skills obsolete.

While many experts are rightly concerned about substitution, a smaller group views this shift from a different perspective: as an opportunity for new skill development. This perspective is best understood through the example of calculators.

When calculators were first introduced in the 1980s, they sparked widespread fear. After all, they allowed anyone—regardless of deep mathematical knowledge—to achieve the same results as someone with a PhD in arithmetic, simply by knowing how to use the tool effectively. This dramatically equalized outcomes, or at the very least, democratized access to solving complex mathematical equations.

Suddenly, performing advanced calculations was no longer limited to a select group of experts who had devoted their lives to studying mathematics; it became a skill accessible to most people.

With AI, the implications are even more profound. For the first time in history, we have a technology that mimics the functioning of the human brain—but on steroids. Unlike previous innovations, AI is not just automating tasks; it is expanding access to a vast range of skills that were once uniquely human—such as learning, decision-making, writing, and creativity. By making complex tasks more accessible and processing vast amounts of information effortlessly, AI is fundamentally reshaping what it means to acquire and apply knowledge.

Fast forward to today's world: we now know that calculators have not eliminated the need to study mathematics—but they have reshaped which skills matter most for mathematicians. The focus has shifted from simply solving problems to understanding and deconstructing them, selecting the right data inputs, and effectively leveraging the tools that calculators provide.

Risk of Dependence

Democratization comes with a trade-off: as AI expands access to skills, it also raises the risk of overdependence—where reliance on technology weakens our ability to think critically and function independently. When technology takes over certain tasks, the very skills it replaces can begin to atrophy. People who become too dependent on technological tools—both in life and at work—may lose the opportunity to develop a deep understanding of the principles behind them, and as a result, their ability to function independently diminishes when access to technology is limited.

Think of what happens all too often at the end of a meal with a large group of friends. When the bill arrives, instead of quickly doing the math in our heads, we instinctively reach for our phones to calculate the split. The convenience of technology has, in many ways, reduced the need for certain types of mental agility, making us worse at performing even simple calculations on our own—something we realize only when our phone battery dies or there's no internet connection.

A recent study by Macnamara and colleagues[2] warns that frequent use of AI assistance can lead to unintended skill degradation—with users often unaware that their abilities are declining. The study highlights how AI-driven decision-making tools, particularly in high-stakes fields like medicine and aviation, can lead professionals to unknowingly lose their expertise over time.

This phenomenon aligns with what AI expert and author Pascal Bornet calls "AI obesity"[3]—a term describing the excessive reliance on AI at the expense of human capabilities. This overdependence is particularly risky because AI is far from perfect: with its biases, ethical concerns, and occasional hallucinations, blindly trusting AI can degrade the quality of our work rather than enhance it.

Much like relying on a calculator without understanding its logic, overreliance on AI can leave us unable to recognize even obvious mistakes. Imagine sending out a critical weekly report to your boss without noticing a glaring error—such as an extra zero in an Excel formula—simply because you didn't double-check the AI-generated output; or not verifying the source of an AI-generated meeting note-taker and unintentionally spreading biased or incorrect information. Without the ability to critically assess AI's results, we risk amplifying its flaws rather than leveraging its strengths.

Research from Carnegie Mellon and Microsoft,[4] conducted with 319 knowledge workers, reinforces this concern. The study found that the more people use AI, the less critical thinking they engage in. A key irony of automation is that by mechanizing routine tasks and leaving exception-handling to the human user, it deprives them of regular opportunities to practice judgment and strengthen cognitive skills, and over time, this leads to mental atrophy, leaving users unprepared to handle complex situations when they inevitably arise.

In our survey, 44% of respondents expressed concern that using AI tools could make them overly dependent on them. This fear echoes the "calculator effect" described above, where reliance on a tool—like calculators in education—raises questions about whether we are losing core skills in the process and highlights the delicate balance between leveraging technology for efficiency and preserving essential human capabilities.

Risk of Commoditization

The challenges associated with the use of AI go beyond the risks of substitution and dependence. Another major concern is commoditization. When AI grants widespread access to the same knowledge, problem-solving abilities, tools, and even ideas, what will set one professional apart from their colleagues? Likewise, if businesses all have access to similar data, algorithms, and AI systems, what will differentiate one company from its competition?

These questions illustrate why standing out becomes increasingly difficult in the age of AI. When everyone has equal access to the same AI tools, traditional skills alone are no longer enough to create a competitive edge. If nearly everyone is adopting AI, simply using these tools without evolving one's skillset adds little value. True differentiation comes not from adoption alone, but from developing new capabilities that complement and enhance AI's potential.

Human Intelligence Versus AI Intelligence

The 2024 Nobel Prizes raise a profound question: Who was the true winner eventually—Human Intelligence or Artificial Intelligence itself? Nobel Prizes are traditionally awarded for human achievement, but in 2024, for the first time, they recognized work that might not have been possible without AI. Were these awards a recognition of human ingenuity in advancing AI, or of AI overcoming human ingenuity?

The answer is complex.

Let's start by saying that yes, the Nobel Prizes were awarded to Human Intelligence—to the ingenuity behind developing AI and applying it to some of the most complex scientific challenges. The distinction, subtle yet crucial, is that the recognition still belongs to the human minds that created and harnessed AI, not to the technology itself, and that it remains a celebration of human brilliance, innovation, and discovery.

But now let's consider the second part of the question. If today, Demis Hassabis and his team at DeepMind were awarded a Nobel Prize in Chemistry for an AI model that accurately predicts protein structures—outperforming human researchers in a task that had stumped scientists for decades—what does that tell us about the role of AI in the future? If AI can solve scientific challenges more efficiently than even the most brilliant human minds, at what point does it stop being a tool and start becoming a true independent contributor to discovery and innovation? Eventually, if AI can improve itself by writing new code, will it be able to generate new AI systems better than human beings do?

These questions are no longer theoretical. As AI takes on an increasingly central role in our world, far beyond the realm of science, the line between human achievement and machine contribution grows ever more blurred. With each new AI breakthrough, our very definitions of intelligence, creativity, and innovation are being reshaped—challenging long-held assumptions about what it means to be good at what we do.

An Exercise in Ancient Greek Translation

To illustrate the path forward—one that allows us to harness AI's potential without being replaced by AI—I want to take a step back in time. Specifically, to my teenage years in Italy, when I was studying Ancient Greek in school.

Picture this: On a chilly winter morning in Italy—the country that gave birth to the Renaissance and proudly upholds a deep-rooted tradition in the humanities—I stepped into a classroom carrying a heavy Ancient Greek dictionary. The room was orderly, with rows of neatly arranged desks facing a blackboard, ready for a group of 14-year-olds embarking on their first year at *Liceo Classico*.

Here, we studied philosophy, literature, Latin, Ancient Greek, and art history, among other disciplines, in preparation for college. It felt like a world apart—yet it was just the year 2000. At the time, the world was undergoing a digital revolution, fueled by the rise of the Internet. Meanwhile, the dot-com bubble was at its peak, sparking a question on everyone's mind: Would digital technologies truly change the world, or was it all just a passing fad?

My teacher, though, was not part of everyone. She was not concerned about that at all. That morning, she had us return to the roots of nearly every modern language, guiding us through the fundamentals of translating an Ancient Greek text. Back then, there was no Google Translate, let alone ChatGPT. I remember flipping through the pages of heavy dictionaries, searching for the Greek words needed to piece together a translation. The real challenge, however, wasn't just finding the right words. Our final grade depended on how natural and coherent our translation sounded—how well it captured the essence of the original text.

I was lucky. In my grandparents' time, they weren't even allowed a dictionary—they had to memorize most words by heart so that their grades depended not only on how well their translation read but also on their ability to recall the words entirely from memory. At least I had the dictionary to assist me. But so did all my classmates.

While my grandparents' final grade reflected both memorization and translation skills, mine was based primarily on my ability to translate. But that raised a new challenge: If everyone had access to the same tool—the dictionary—how could I stand out?

First, it came down to how effectively I used the dictionary. Not everyone approached it the same way. Some were faster; some were slower. Some relied on it mechanically, while others navigated it more strategically. But beyond that, differentiation came from how well the final translation flowed: creativity, contextual interpretation, and the subtle human touch all played a role in setting one translation apart from another.

As I lugged those heavy Latin and Greek dictionaries around, I often asked myself, "Why? Why study ancient languages that are no longer in use? Why memorize so many translation rules by heart?" At the time, AI was mostly confined to academic discussions and was far from mainstream, but even the bulky mainframe computer we had at home made me suspicious that things would change. It seemed inevitable that one day, the way through which we would study these languages might become obsolete. So, what would *studying* Ancient Greek look like in the age of AI?

With the rise of generative AI tools, particularly after the launch of ChatGPT in 2022, one of the first things that came to mind was to test its capabilities—specifically, to see if it could translate the same Ancient Greek text from my high school final exam in 2004, the *Maturità*. I remember having four hours to complete the exam, and I barely made it. I spent nearly three hours and fifty minutes meticulously translating the text, leaving myself only the last 10 minutes to review it. Many of my classmates didn't even finish in time.

The process was grueling, requiring intense focus, patience, and a deep understanding of the language.

For context, the text I had to translate for my *Maturità* exam was an excerpt from Plato titled "The Long Journey of Humanity Toward Civil Coexistence." The passage comes from Protagoras's speech in Plato's *Protagoras*, where he recounts the myth of Prometheus and the origins of human civilization.

In its original Ancient Greek, it looked like this:

Επειδη δε ο ανθρωπος θειας μετεσχε μοιρας, πρωτον μεν δια την του θεου συγγενειαν ζωων μονον θεους ενομισεν, και επεχειρει βωμους τε ιδρυεσθαι και αγαλματα θεων: επειτα φωνην και ονοματα ταχυ διηρθρωσατο τη τεχνη, και οικησεις και εσθητας και υπο δεσεις και στρωμνας και τας εκ γης τροφας ηυρετο. Ουτω δη παρεσκευασμενοι κατ' αρχας ανθρωποι ωκουν σποραδην, πολεις δε ουκ ησαν: απωλλυντο ουν υπο των θηριων δια το πανταχη αυτων ασθενεστεροι ειναι, και η δημιουργικη τεχνη αυτοις προς μεν τροφην ικανη βοηθος ην, προς δε τον των θηριων πολεμον ενδεης - πολιτικην γαρ τεχνην ουπω ειχον, ης μερος πολεμικη - εζητουν δη αθροιζεσθαι και σωζεσθαι κτιζοντες πολεις: οτ' ουν αθροισθειεν, ηδικουν αλληλους ατε ουκ εχοντες την πολιτικην τεχνην, ωστε παλιν σκεδαννυμενοι διεφθειροντο.

Almost 20 years later, I decided to put AI to the test. I asked ChatGPT:

If you were an 18-year-old Italian student taking the prova di maturità and wanted to get the highest grade, how would you translate the following text from Ancient Greek to English?

The result was mind-blowing:

Since man partook in a divine nature, he was, first of all, the only living being to conceive the idea of gods due to his kinship with the divine. Thus, he began to build altars and statues in their honor. Then, with the aid of his craft, he swiftly articulated speech and created names, and he invented dwellings, clothing, footwear, bedding, and means of sustenance derived from the earth.

At first, however, human beings lived scattered, without cities; as a result, they were being annihilated by wild beasts, for they were weaker than them in every way. Their technical skills provided sufficient aid for survival but were inadequate for waging war against the beasts, since they had not yet acquired the art of politics, of which warfare is a part. Consequently, they sought to gather together and ensure their safety by building cities. However, once assembled, they began harming one another, as they lacked the knowledge of political organization; thus, they dispersed again and continued to perish.

The first particularly interesting thing I noted is how this excerpt—perhaps a premonition—serves as a powerful analogy between fire and AI. Just as Prometheus gave fire to humans, granting them the ability to transform their environment and propel civilization forward, we could say that AI is our modern-day fire. It is a tool of immense power, capable of elevating humanity to new heights, yet one that also carries profound existential challenges. In the passage, early humans lacked political wisdom, leading to chaos and destruction when they gathered. The same pattern is emerging with AI today: we have incredibly powerful tools—Large Language Models, automation, predictive analytics—but without clear regulations, ethical frameworks, and governance, these technologies risk causing more harm than good.

The lesson from this passage is not just about survival but about the crucial role of wisdom in handling powerful tools. AI, much like Prometheus's fire, is neither inherently good nor bad; its impact depends entirely on how we use it. If we fail to establish a guiding framework, much like the *art of politics* in the myth, we risk plunging into disorder rather than progress.

The second thing that truly impressed me was the speed at which AI translated the passage—roughly 10 seconds. And you know what? It sounded pretty good. I'd give it a solid 9 out of 10. "Why wasn't ChatGPT around back then?" I couldn't help but think as I reviewed the AI-generated translation. With nearly four hours left on the clock, I could have spent all that time refining the text, ensuring every sentence flowed naturally, and aiming for a perfect score. Because yes, some parts of the AI translation sounded slightly off—but the same was true for my original translation. The difference was that I didn't have the luxury of time to refine mine. Although I ended up getting a very good grade, I could have done much better with the use of AI.

The key learning from this story is that the best outcomes from using tools that not only outperform human skills but also operate at greater speed come from the combination of two factors. First, whenever we have a tool—whether it's something as simple as a dictionary or as sophisticated as AI—what ultimately sets us apart isn't the tool itself, but how well we use it. If everyone has access to the same technology, the real differentiator lies in how effectively we leverage it.

Second, the final outcome of any tool, no matter how advanced, is shaped by the human contribution we add to it. A tool can assist, enhance, or even take over parts of a task, but its true impact depends on the creativity, judgment, and refinement we bring to the output—often using the time saved by the tool to elevate the final result.

A New Skills Paradigm

By automating and augmenting many of our tasks, AI not only saves us time but also reduces our reliance on technical skills. This shift presents an opportunity—or perhaps even a necessity—to develop and refine human skills that were previously overlooked. These skills were often deprioritized because they were difficult to measure, time-consuming to develop, and perceived as inefficient in traditional work environments.

AI is ushering in a new skills paradigm—one we call the *hybrid skillset*. To thrive in this evolving landscape, professionals and leaders must urgently adapt by developing two complementary sets of skills: on the one hand, *AI literacy skills* that make us effectively leverage AI tools, navigate their complexities, and maximize their potential; on the other hand, *human literacy skills*—the uniquely human capabilities that AI's efficiency allows us to focus on, such as critical thinking, creativity, empathy, and decision-making.

This shift is not just about technology—it's about us, humans. The professionals, leaders, and individuals who choose to master both AI literacy and human literacy will shape the future. The rest? They risk becoming relics of the past—outpaced not by machines, but by those who understand how to work alongside them.

To understand and develop these skills, we must first map out a fundamental question: What does AI now do *better* than humans, and what will remain uniquely human?

The End of Human Uniqueness?

Between February and July 2024, researchers conducted a simulation[5] involving 344 participants facing real-world decisions typically made by industry CEOs. These decisions were based on historical pricing, market shifts, sales trends, and disruptions like COVID-19.

Participants were up against a powerful opponent: OpenAI's GPT-4o, the latest version of its LLM. The goal of the game was simple: while maximizing market capitalization, survive as long as possible without being fired by a virtual board.

The results were striking: GPT-4o consistently outperformed human participants, designing products with cost efficiency, responding swiftly to market signals, and achieving greater profitability three rounds ahead of the top human performer.

These findings are consistent with what Scott Aaronson, professor of Computer Science at the University of Texas, explained in his keynote address at TEDx Palo Alto.[6] He highlighted what he sees as "the problem with human specialness in the age of AI"—namely, that for any task with a reasonably objective measure of success or failure, such as games, competitions, or structured challenges, AI will inevitably match or surpass human performance.

In the OpenAI GPT-4o simulation, AI did struggle with outlier events like COVID-19—highlighting the fact that AI's success depends on the availability of past data patterns.

But according to Aaronson, "Given any task with a reasonably objective metric of success or failure, and on which an AI can be given suitably many examples of success and failure, it's only a matter of years before not only AI, but AI on our current paradigm, will match or beat human performance." In other words, if a task can be quantified and AI has access to sufficient training data, its dominance over humans is just a matter of time. Aaronson refers to this inevitability as the "Game Over Theory."

As humans, it has been years since we had any hope of outperforming AI in games like chess and Go—milestones that are now well behind us—and it's only a matter of time before AI surpasses human performance in other competitive domains, such as the Mathematics Olympiad. GPT-4, for instance, can pass the Uniform Bar Examination with ease, scoring in the top 10% of test takers. It can also answer 90% of questions correctly on the U.S. Medical Licensing Examination. By the time you're reading this book, AI will likely have achieved even more advanced feats.

AI in Cancer Diagnosis[7]

Scientists at Harvard Medical School have developed a versatile, ChatGPT-like AI model capable of performing a wide range of diagnostic tasks across multiple forms of cancer. Named CHIEF, this AI system goes beyond typical models that are trained for specific tasks, such as detecting the presence of cancer or predicting a tumor's genetic profile. Using 15 million unlabeled images, CHIEF was tested on 19 cancer types and outperformed existing models across 11 datasets.

With an accuracy rate nearing 94%, CHIEF exemplifies how general-purpose AI is expanding beyond narrow tasks—tackling complex problems that once required highly specialized human expertise.

Differences in Operating Strengths

But how do we determine if AI is better than we are in fields like writing, the humanities, or creativity, where there are no reasonably objective metrics of success? Measuring performance in these areas isn't straightforward—there's a high degree of subjectivity involved. For example, would you say your writing is better than ChatGPT's? What would your friends, readers, or family say? (Though let's be honest, your mom doesn't count—she's always going to say your writing is better.)

To some extent, rather than asking which is *better*, it may be more useful to explore the differences in *how* each operates. If AI is transforming the way we work and think, how do its capabilities compare to those of human intelligence?

The table below maps out the differences between human and artificial intelligence across key cognitive and functional domains, illustrating how humans and AI process information, make decisions, and interact with the world. Understanding these distinctions can help us better navigate the evolving relationship between humans and AI.

Domain	Human Intelligence	Artificial Intelligence
Decision-Making	Humans make decisions using reasoning (deductive, inductive, and abductive), intuition, and experience. Decision-making is influenced by emotions, biases (e.g., confirmation bias, availability heuristic), and contextual understanding.	AI makes decisions through logical, data-driven models such as decision trees and neural networks. It follows consistent patterns based on data but may inherit biases from training datasets. It lacks human-like intuition and contextual adaptability.
Creativity	Human creativity emerges from emotional experience, cultural influences, and the ability to connect unrelated ideas. It is shaped by curiosity, intrinsic motivation, and personal expression.	AI generates creative outputs (e.g., music, art, and text) using algorithms trained on large datasets. While it can replicate patterns and styles, it lacks intrinsic motivation, originality, and emotional depth.

Domain	Human Intelligence	Artificial Intelligence
Learning	Humans learn through experience, observation, trial and error, and social interactions. Learning is adaptable, requires minimal data, and generalizes across different contexts.	AI learns by processing large datasets through supervised, unsupervised, or reinforcement learning. It requires extensive data, struggles to generalize outside its training set, and lacks experiential learning.
IQ-Related Tasks	Humans demonstrate intelligence through logical reasoning, verbal comprehension, problem-solving, and abstract thinking. Performance on IQ tests is influenced by education, culture, and prior knowledge.	AI can outperform humans in IQ-related tasks such as pattern recognition, logical reasoning, and mathematical problem-solving. However, its intelligence is narrow, task-specific, and lacks generalized understanding.
Task Execution	Human task performance is influenced by cognitive load, physical limitations, time constraints, and external distractions.	AI executes tasks with near-limitless efficiency, constrained only by computational power. It can process vast amounts of data rapidly but lacks adaptability beyond predefined parameters.

(*continued*)

(continued)

Domain	Human Intelligence	Artificial Intelligence
Content Production	Humans create content based on personal experiences, emotions, and cultural context. Writing, storytelling, and artistic expression are deeply influenced by intention and creativity.	AI generates text, images, and media based on training data and structured prompts. While it can mimic human language and style, it lacks true intent, emotional nuance, and original thought.
Emotional Intelligence	Humans possess self-awareness, empathy, emotional regulation, and social adaptability. These skills are critical for leadership, communication, and interpersonal relationships.	AI can analyze sentiment and detect emotions using affective computing but does not experience emotions. Its responses are simulated and lack genuine empathy or self-awareness.
Social Cognition	Humans understand social dynamics, read nonverbal cues, and infer the mental states of others. Social cognition is essential for building relationships and navigating complex interactions.	AI can simulate social interactions (e.g., chatbots, virtual assistants) but lacks genuine understanding of human emotions, intentions, and social complexities. Its interactions are scripted and rule-based.

Domain	Human Intelligence	Artificial Intelligence
Trust-Building	Humans build trust through relationships, consistency, emotional connection, and social experiences. Trust is dynamic and influenced by past interactions and context.	AI does not inherently build trust but earns it through transparency, reliability, and accuracy. Trust in AI depends on explainability and the absence of bias rather than emotional or relational factors.
Perception	Humans integrate sensory information seamlessly, influenced by experience, emotions, and cognitive biases. Perception is adaptable but prone to illusions and misinterpretations.	AI excels in processing images, recognizing patterns, and analyzing audio through advanced algorithms. However, it struggles with ambiguous, incomplete, or conflicting sensory information and lacks holistic multisensory perception.

While this comparison highlights key differences between Human Intelligence and Artificial Intelligence, determining which is better at a given task is not always straightforward. Many skills exist on a spectrum—some have objective measures of success, while others are deeply subjective.

Skills with inherently subjective success criteria are not only less susceptible to automation but are also becoming more valuable in the age of AI. In fields like mathematics, games, and many aspects of business, performance is measured by clear-cut metrics—either you solve the problem or you don't; either you win or you lose. However, in areas such as business strategy, writing, art, and music—where creativity and personal expression take center stage—the concept of *better* is far more fluid. It is shaped by individual preferences, cultural context, and the inherent subjectivity of human taste.

Hard and Soft Skills in the Age of AI

It's no coincidence that the distinction between objective and subjective AI outcomes aligns with the divide between two major skill categories: hard skills and soft skills. And it is no coincidence that in the age of AI, the balance between these two is shifting dramatically.

In 1968, the upper ranks of the U.S. Army faced a pressing challenge: certain factors were directly influencing the success of military units, yet these elements were neither measured nor accounted for in training programs, development plans, or performance evaluations.

In other words, something intangible within battalion structures was shaping soldier behavior—at times fostering dedication and cohesion, at other times fueling internal conflicts or disrupting the flow of critical information between units. This unseen force was deeply affecting both the performance of officers and the outcomes of missions, yet it remained unquantified, unstructured, and unaddressed.

Lacking a precise definition, the Army's top minds launched a rigorous academic effort to categorize these complex, intangible abilities. They labeled them *soft skills*—a stark contrast to the easily measurable *hard skills* like driving a vehicle, operating a machine gun, or preparing a logistics report.

Despite acknowledging the undeniable value of soft skills—such as the ability to inspire, build trust, or think flexibly—Army scholars struggled to develop concrete methods for identifying, measuring, and teaching them. The following traits have traditionally made soft skills more challenging to prioritize than hard skills:

1. **Broad (vs. hard skills, which are specific).** Unlike hard skills, which are task-oriented and tailored to specific functions, soft skills are universally applicable across various business and life situations. Their versatility makes them indispensable for navigating complex environments, adapting to different contexts, and fostering effective human collaboration.

2. **Difficult to transfer (vs. hard skills, which are easier to teach and transfer).** While technical skills can be systematically taught and passed down, allowing one person to directly help another acquire the same ability, soft skills are far more personal and internal. Their development relies less on formal

instruction and more on individual growth, lived experiences, and self-awareness, making them harder to replicate or standardize.

3. **Difficult to measure (vs. hard skills, which are quantifiable).** Assessing a software developer's coding proficiency or a candidate's fluency in English is relatively straightforward since hard skills come with clear metrics, tests, and benchmarks. In contrast, evaluating someone's ability to collaborate, demonstrate empathy, or think critically is far more complex. Soft skills lack standardized measurement tools, making it challenging for organizations to assess and develop them effectively.

Paradoxically, despite the undeniable importance of soft skills, we often gravitate toward objective, quantifiable targets simply because they are clearer and leave little room for ambiguity. Unlike behavioral goals—where success can feel vague or subjective—numeric targets provide a sense of certainty, making them easier to track and evaluate, but this preference for clarity often comes at the cost of overlooking the skills that truly drive long-term success.

Soft Skills in Practice: A Normal Day at the Office

Your manager calls you in for an end-of-year feedback session to set goals for the upcoming year. They start with the easy part— clear, quantifiable targets like "achieve 15% sales growth in Q1." These are concrete, measurable, and straightforward to track.

But then comes a different kind of objective: "Your goal this year is to be more collaborative." You nod politely, thank her, and walk out of the room—only to feel a wave of uncertainty.

What does being more collaborative actually mean? How do you show it? How do you measure where you stand today, or by how much you need to improve? And most important, how do you develop that skill in the first place?

Because they are so broad, difficult to teach, and hard to measure, soft skills have traditionally been deprioritized in the workplace—an inheritance of the Industrial Revolution mindset that prioritizes efficiency, growth, and maximized outcomes. However, in the age of AI, the very fact that soft skills are difficult to quantify doesn't make them less important—it makes them *more* important, as these skills are precisely what make humans complementary to AI rather than replaceable by it. As AI automates technical tasks and accelerates decision-making, the ability to think critically, collaborate, and bring emotional intelligence to problem-solving will be what truly sets us apart.

Data from our survey reinforce this point: 82% of respondents said they would prefer to hire a candidate who lacks sufficient hard skills for the role but has strong soft skills, rather than the opposite. When asked why, two reasons stood out in their comments. First, unsurprisingly, respondents noted that hard skills are much easier to teach and develop than soft skills. But the second reason is more surprising: as companies increasingly adopt AI tools, many hard skills are being automated and replaced by machines, while soft skills remain uniquely human and irreplaceable.

Why IQ Isn't Enough Anymore

This shift in focus—from hard skills to soft—was not always obvious to me. I grew up in a world that taught me the exact opposite—that my focus should be on developing strong hard skills, often measured by Intellectual Quotient (IQ) tests, while soft skills were rarely mentioned, let alone prioritized.

That lasted up until I read Daniel Goleman's *Emotional Intelligence*,[8] a book that completely shifted my perspective. It introduced me to the idea that while IQ may provide an early advantage, its influence diminishes over time: once inside the workplace, success depends far more on emotional intelligence (EI).

The transition from academia to the professional world makes this clear. In school, success is determined by structured tests, clear-cut problems, and individual performance. But the workplace is far more complex—an unpredictable environment where ambiguity is the norm. Projects shift, stakeholders have conflicting interests, crises emerge unexpectedly, and success is determined not just by what you know, but by how well you navigate relationships, communicate effectively, and manage your emotions under pressure.

This is where IQ's limitations become apparent. High cognitive ability might help process information quickly or solve complex analytical problems, but it does little to address the human side of work. In a world where collaboration, negotiation, and adaptability are essential, interpersonal skills often outweigh raw intellectual horsepower.

Enter emotional intelligence: unlike IQ, which remains relatively stable, EI is a skill that can be developed and refined. Research consistently shows EI as a key predictor of workplace success, particularly in roles that require teamwork, leadership, and high levels of interaction.

Two studies highlight this point. David McClelland's 1998 study, "Identifying Competencies with Behavioral-Event Interviews,"[9] found that while cognitive and technical skills are necessary to enter many professions, emotional competencies are what truly distinguish top performers, especially in leadership. Similarly, Sigal Barsade and Olivia O'Neill's 2014 study, "What's Love Got to Do with It?"[10] revealed that teams with high collective EI exhibited greater cooperation, higher creativity, and overall better performance—demonstrating that EI is not just essential for individual success but also for building strong organizational cultures.

These insights heavily influenced Goleman's work and are even more relevant in today's AI-driven world. If IQ serves as the foundation for technical skills, EI is the fertile ground for socio-emotional skills—where, as we have established, humans still hold a decisive advantage over AI. When these human literacy skills are paired with AI literacy skills, they form the core of a new paradigm for thriving in the age of AI.

Thinking, Acting, and Feeling: The Core of What Makes Us Human

To define the new skills required to thrive in the age of Artificial Intelligence—what we have called the *hybrid skillset*—we must begin by examining the core activities that have always defined human existence. Not specific tasks like cooking, writing poetry, or filling out an Excel spreadsheet—these vary from person to person. Instead, we need to focus on the fundamental, universal activities that all humans engage in. No exceptions. At our core, we do three main things: we think, we act, and we feel.

First, *thinking* encompasses our cognitive processes—reasoning, analyzing, imagining, problem-solving, and decision-making. It's how we process information, plan, and make sense of the world around us. It's also how we generate creative ideas and find solutions to problems. We engage in thinking constantly. A study[11] by psychology researchers at Queen's University in Canada, which analyzed brain scans, found that the average person has more than 6,000 thoughts per day, which is why it is so hard to get into that meditative state of "no thoughts"—our brains are wired to constantly generate new thoughts.

Second, *acting* involves the execution of plans, initiatives, and behaviors that produce tangible outcomes. It's about transforming thoughts into reality—creating tools, building systems, interacting with the environment, and bringing ideas to life. However, this is where a common challenge arises: the *insight–action gap*. While generating thoughts is effortless, acting on them is far more complex. Action requires effort, carries risks, and is often constrained by external factors. This gap explains why many ideas never materialize—because turning intention into execution is a far greater challenge than simply thinking about it.

Third, *feeling* encompasses emotions, intuition, and subjective experiences. It's how we connect with ourselves and others; process emotions like joy, fear, love, and sadness; and navigate interpersonal relationships. Feeling also plays a crucial role in self-awareness, shaping our perceptions, decisions, and interactions with the world around us.

Obviously, these three macro activities rarely function in isolation—they are deeply interconnected. Thoughts influence feelings, feelings drive actions, and actions, in turn, generate new thoughts and emotions. Likewise, decisions made by our brains often (though not always) translate into actions.

At any given moment, as long as we are alive, we are engaged in one or a combination of these three dimensions. Unlike external circumstances—such as wealth, social status, or age—these fundamental activities remain constant. Whether rich or poor, young or old, part of one culture or another, we all think, act, and feel. Even if we renounce all material possessions and embrace a secluded monastic life, we are still bound to these three forces. They represent, in essence, what it means to be human.

It is no different in the workplace. Regardless of our role, industry, company size, or seniority level, these three human dimensions— thinking, acting, and feeling—are constantly at play. We think creatively during brainstorming sessions to generate original ideas, analyze data to determine the best strategy, and predict emerging business trends that could shape our industry.

We act by executing tasks, implementing strategies, and delivering tangible results. Whether coding software, assembling products, or presenting a business case, this dimension is where ideas and plans take form. Action is the backbone of progress—it's what transforms strategy into reality.

And although many might argue that there's little room for feeling in the workplace, they couldn't be more wrong. We feel when we make intuitive decisions based on a gut instinct, when we seek to understand customer behavior through empathetic conversations, and when we navigate team dynamics and workplace culture. Feeling is embedded in trust, engagement, and motivation—the driving forces behind both individual and collective success. It shapes how we lead, collaborate, and resolve conflicts, making emotional intelligence an essential component of any thriving professional environment.

The Hybrid Skillset Framework

As we stand at the intersection of Human Intelligence and Artificial Intelligence, it becomes clear that success in this new era will not come from competing with AI in areas where AI excels, but from complementing AI use with skills that remain uniquely human. The way forward is not about choosing between AI and human expertise—it is about integrating both into a new hybrid set of skills that leverages the best of each.

This is where the Hybrid Skillset comes into play. Rather than being a single set of competencies, the hybrid skillset is best understood as a dynamic interplay of cognitive, behavioral, and emotional abilities—skills that enable professionals to work effectively alongside AI. To make this framework more actionable, we can break it down into three core pillars:

- **Cognitive Hybrid Skills:** AI can better process data, but humans must define the right problems, contextualize information, and generate original ideas. This requires expertise in skills like Prompting, Data Sensemaking, and Reperception (see Section I)—skills that ensure AI's outputs are meaningful and relevant.
- **Behavioral Hybrid Skills:** AI is efficient in executing tasks but lacks adaptability and true innovation. Humans must embrace skills like Augmentation, Adaptability, and Antifragility (see Section II)—allowing AI to handle routine tasks while focusing on experimentation and learning from uncertainty.
- **Emotional Hybrid Skills:** AI can recognize patterns in emotions but does not feel, empathize, or build deep trust. The most enduring human advantage will lie in skills like Empathy, Trust, and Agency (see Section III), as businesses and leaders recognize that emotional intelligence is the true differentiator in an AI-driven world.

The table below maps out key human activities across cognitive, behavioral, and emotional dimensions, illustrating the degree to which AI can be a substitute for these tasks, what AI does best, and where human strengths remain indispensable. It also highlights the critical skills professionals must develop to effectively collaborate with AI—ensuring that we don't just adopt new technology but actively shape its role in our work and decision-making.

Pillar	Human Activity	What AI Does Best	What Humans Do Better	Key Skill	Definition	Associated Behaviors
Cognitivez	Learning	Processes vast data, identifies patterns, retrieves knowledge	Prioritizes key info, defines questions, applies context	**Prompting**	Interacting effectively with AI through precise, structured inputs	Asking strategic, well-crafted questions to get optimal outputs
	Decision-Making	Analyzes data, finds correlations, predicts outcomes	Applies intuition, ethics, judgment	**Data Sensemaking**	Critically assessing AI output to extract meaningful, actionable insights	Evaluating recommendations through strategic and ethical lenses
	Idea Generation	Synthesizes knowledge, optimizes patterns	Integrates diverse experiences, has cognitive flexibility	**Reperception**	Seeing problems from new angles, challenging assumptions, finding new connections	Reframing challenges, generating novel perspectives

(continued)

(*continued*)

Pillar	Human Activity	What AI Does Best	What Humans Do Better	Key Skill	Definition	Associated Behaviors
Behavioral	Performing Familiar Tasks	Automates high-volume, familiar and repetitive tasks	Enhances strategy, brings quality and nuance	Augmentation	Leveraging AI to improve—rather than just replace—human work	Using AI for efficiency while adding critical oversight
	Performing Unfamiliar Tasks	Predicts change using past data	Adapts flexibly, improvises, handles complexity	Adaptability	Adjusting rapidly to new conditions and staying effective under pressure	Leading through uncertainty, making decisions in gray areas
	Innovation	Improves iteratively within defined frameworks	Thrives in uncertainty, learns from failure	Antifragility	Minimize cost of mistakes and maximize the learning from them	Embracing failure, experimenting quickly, and learning from mistakes

Pillar	Human Activity	What AI Does Best	What Humans Do Better	Key Skill	Definition	Associated Behaviors
Emotional	Connection	Detects emotional patterns, simulates responses	Feels, empathizes, and expresses emotion authentically	**Empathy**	Understanding and sharing others' emotional states	Active listening, emotional attunement, compassionate feedback
	Collaboration	Coordinates communication, schedules workflows	Builds trust, navigates team dynamics	**Trust**	Creating psychological safety and relational credibility	Demonstrating integrity, reliability, emotional presence
	Ethics	Goal maximization but without self-awareness or conscience	Ethical concerns limit goal maximization based on self-awareness and conscience	**Agency**	Taking accountability for its own actions, even if we cannot control them	Applying ethical standards to the use of AI

The reality is that AI will continue to advance, and the line between what it does best and what we do best will keep shifting. But the key to staying ahead is not resisting AI—it is mastering how to work with it. Those who develop a Hybrid Skillset will not only future-proof their careers but redefine the workplace in ways we are only beginning to imagine.

This book is a roadmap to mastering this skillset transformation. In the next chapters, we will explore how organizations and individuals can actively cultivate these skills—and what it takes to thrive in a world where AI is no longer just a threat, but a superpower to make us thrive in the workplace.

SECTION

I

Cognitive Transformation

2

Prompting

UNDER THE BRIGHT Athenian sun, in the Greek agora of 399 BCE, a restless crowd gathered to watch the city's most provocative thinker stand trial. The charges were extremely serious: impiety against the Gods (*asebeia* in Greek) and corruption of the youth of Athens. The thinker standing trial was Socrates—a philosopher whose defiant questioning of truth and virtue would echo through the ages, immortalized by the writings of his disciples Plato and Xenophon.

Socrates had a habit of questioning the norms and structures of Athenian democracy—a practice that made him a dangerous figure to those in power—through his signature philosophical approach: what became known as the Socratic method. Through relentless questioning, he dismantled assumptions, challenged dogmas, and exposed contradictions—often revealing the ignorance of Athens' most influential figures. In some sense, he was sentenced for "asking too many questions." He ultimately was condemned to death, and his execution—carried out with a lethal dose of hemlock—was the ultimate price he paid for his relentless pursuit of truth.

Just as Socrates's questioning challenged the power structures of ancient Athens, it also became a tool—not only for himself, but for anyone seeking to break free from rigid beliefs and challenge the status quo. After all, the true seeds of learning, change, and innovation lie not in having the right answers, but in asking the right questions. The same is even truer today: in an era where machines already possess more knowledge and answers than we do—and where AI has democratized access to hard skills that once took years to develop—the real key to unlocking AI's power is our ability to ask better questions.

Nearly 2,500 years after Socrates's death, little has changed. While we no longer prosecute people for questioning authority, the systems around us—schools, universities, corporations—still reward answers over curiosity. In her study "The Business Case for Curiosity,"[1] Francesca Gino, from Harvard Business School, surveyed over 3,000 employees across industries and found that only 24% reported feeling curious in their jobs regularly, while nearly 70% said they face barriers to asking more questions at work.

Curiosity as a Driver of Growth

Why is questioning undervalued? Historically, knowledge was scarce, and possessing it gave its holder a competitive edge. With the Industrial Revolution, efficiency was valued over inquiry—training workers to follow procedures, not challenge them—and many organizations still operate under this legacy today. Add to that human ego: in hierarchical environments, questions can feel like threats, exposing gaps in knowledge or authority. It's safer not to ask. Fear of appearing ignorant or incompetent keeps people silent, wondering, "What will others think of me if I ask this question?"

Growing up in Italy, I was naturally curious, often challenging my teachers with a critical mindset—and lots of questions. Yet I quickly realized that questioning was neither encouraged nor well received, and most of the time dismissed as a waste of time. As my experience reflects, most education systems reward having the right answers over asking meaningful questions, teaching us that certainty—not curiosity—is the key to success.

But as Michel Chouinard's study "Children's Questions: A Mechanism for Cognitive Development"[2] shows, children naturally ask more questions than adults to make sense of the world—and this curiosity is a key driver of cognitive growth.

No story illustrates this better than the invention of the Polaroid camera. Picture this: A father on vacation snaps a photo of his four-year-old daughter and, immediately after, she innocently asks,

"Dad, can I see the picture now?" Today, we'd think nothing of it—anyone would simply pull out their smartphone and show the photo. But it was 1944, and the idea was absurd: developing photos required a trip to a lab, a darkroom, and a trained technician. So the father explained, "Sweetheart, there's no way to see the picture right away. It takes time and special equipment." But that simple, almost naïve question stuck with him. Why couldn't photos be developed instantly? Why did the process have to be so complicated? The father wasn't just any parent—he was Edwin Land, the inventor and eventual founder of Polaroid. Inspired by his daughter's question, he went on to invent instant photography.

Now ask yourself: Would any seasoned engineer, expert, or executive in the photo industry have asked that same question? Surely not. They already "knew" the answer. Their expertise, paradoxically, would have limited their curiosity—and that's the trap we fall into every day. But when we don't prioritize asking questions, we fail to develop the very skill that allows us to make the best use of AI's infinite repository of knowledge and hard skills.

AI's Infinite Reservoir of Skills

The main issue with the "anti-Socratic method" is that it was developed in a world where knowledge—and access to new skills—was scarce. It made sense in the past, when scholars, merchants, or navigators who possessed exclusive knowledge of trade routes, medical treatments, or innovations could dominate their fields. Breakthroughs did occur—most notably Johannes Gutenberg's invention of the printing press in 1436, which revolutionized the spread of information. But it wasn't until the twentieth century that the flow of knowledge truly accelerated: Mass media, computers, and eventually the Internet dismantled the barriers that once restricted ideas. Knowledge, once limited to a privileged few, became accessible to millions—and along with it came the opportunity to learn and develop new skills much more easily.

Today, that access has reached an entirely new level. AI is rapidly surpassing human capabilities in acquiring, processing, and applying knowledge—at a scale and speed beyond anything we have seen before.

Generative AI models like GPT-4 have been trained on a volume of data equivalent to billions of books, articles, and online content, having reportedly processed approximately 13 trillion tokens—small chunks of text such as words or word fragments—amounting to roughly 10 trillion words. No human, no matter how intelligent or dedicated, could absorb this much information in a lifetime. As a consequence, AI's breadth of knowledge is unmatched, and it continues to expand as models improve AI's performance and as training sets increase in size.

AI's dominance in knowledge is not just about scale—it's also about speed. While humans spend years studying and practicing to master a field, AI can absorb and process massive amounts of information in a fraction of that time. A law student might spend a decade specializing in corporate law, while AI can analyze decades' worth of legal cases in a matter of seconds. A medical researcher might spend years reviewing clinical trials, but AI can scan thousands of research papers in minutes. Additionally, AI systems don't experience fatigue, cognitive overload, or distractions; unlike humans, who require rest and struggle with maintaining focus over long periods, AI can work around the clock, constantly refining its knowledge.

As a result, the marginal cost of accessing hard skills that require lots of knowledge, training, and learning—like coding, data analysis, or foreign languages—is rapidly approaching zero: it's essentially the cost of having access to, and using, an AI tool. In this reality, where even non-experts can tap into vast knowledge with a simple question or input, our competitive edge no longer lies in what we know, but in how well we ask questions. The better we "question" AI tools, the better we can leverage their virtually limitless knowledge to perform tasks faster and more effectively than we ever could.

Our survey results support this thesis. When asked, "Would you rather work with a colleague who is highly knowledgeable but does not use AI tools, or someone who may not have all the answers but effectively leverages AI?"—59% chose the latter. Their reasoning was clear: as AI exponentially enhances access to knowledge, specific skills become less of a competitive advantage. What becomes essential in this evolving landscape is prompting—namely, the ability to ask better questions to improve the quality of the outputs obtained through AI.

What Is *Prompting?*

In the world of AI, *prompting* refers to the skill of giving clear, specific instructions to guide AI's response. A prompt can take the form of a question, command, or statement—it's the input you provide to get the output you want. Think of it like giving directions: the more precise and well-structured your prompt, the more useful and relevant AI's answer will be, and the more effectively AI can assist us in accessing knowledge, analyzing data, performing tasks, and generating content and creative ideas.

Jane Fraser, CEO of Citi, in an interview with *Fortune*, highlighted the growing importance of this ability in the AI era, stating, "In the world of AI, access to information has become a commodity, and consequently, the differentiator is the ability to craft good prompts."[3]

But prompting isn't just a technical skill for interacting with machines—it's equally powerful when applied to humans. Thoughtful, well-placed questions can challenge assumptions, shift perspectives, and encourage deeper reflection. In the workplace, the ability to ask better questions inspires teams to see problems differently, sparking innovation and fresh solutions; here, AI makes "the impossible possible" (a concept we will revisit in Chapter 4). In a broader sense, prompting also involves the art of asking strategic, meaningful questions that drive reflection and meaningful change—an art mastered over 2,000 years ago by Socrates, who used probing inquiries to challenge beliefs and push people toward deeper understanding.

As we shall see, well-crafted prompts can maximize the quality of AI outputs. But let's first revisit the example of calculators: they didn't just democratize access to complex math—they shifted the advantage. It was no longer about who was naturally better at math, but about who knew how to use the tool effectively. In other words, success wasn't reserved anymore for the smartest or most knowledgeable, but for those who understood how to get the most out of the calculator. We are now witnessing a similar transformation with AI.

Effectively using AI tools allows non-experts to compete directly with experts in almost any field. A professional with no legal background can review complex contracts with obscure data privacy clauses—often more efficiently than a generalist lawyer.

Similarly, a marketing specialist without formal design training can use Generative AI tools like Midjourney to create visuals that rival, or even surpass, those of experienced designers.

Where does the real differentiator lie? Just like with calculators in the 1980s, the advantage isn't in having access to the tool—since everyone does—but in knowing how to use it effectively through precise and smarter inputs.

The most comprehensive study done on AI prompting is "The Prompt Report,"[4] by a group of experts from the University of Maryland, OpenAI, Stanford, Microsoft, Princeton, and other major organizations. They examined 1,565 relevant papers and presented a curated list of 58 text-based prompting techniques, highlighting an important insight: the way you structure and deliver a prompt is as important as what you are asking the AI to do.

The Three Essential Elements of a Good Prompt

The key takeaway of "The Prompt Report" is that prompting AI is not just a technical skill; it is a strategic one. The clarity, specificity, and context of a prompt directly impact both the quality of AI's output and the efficiency of the process. In particular, the elements that make for good prompts are (1) role assignment, (2) clarity and specificity, and (3) context and background.

Role Assignment

AI can take on virtually any persona, profession, or perspective—it's just a matter of specifying it clearly in your prompt. A simple but powerful way to refine prompts is to ask the AI tool to adopt a specific role before making a request, which helps shape its output, making responses more relevant and targeted. Without this guidance, AI may provide generic or unstructured responses that don't fully align with your specific expectations.

For example, imagine you need help drafting a report summarizing key business trends for your team. If you simply ask, "Summarize the latest business trends," the AI tool might provide a broad, high-level response. But if you first specify, "Act as if you are an external consultant summarizing the latest business trends," AI will adjust its response—providing an original external perspective, industry-specific data, and an executive-friendly summary—as an external consultant would. By assigning roles, you guide AI to think within a defined way of thinking, ensuring responses are more tailored, insightful, and useful for your needs.

Clarity and Specificity

Vague or overly broad prompts often lead to generic or irrelevant responses. To ensure AI delivers useful and precise outputs, it's important to clearly define what you're looking for and any relevant constraints.

For example, if you ask, "Write a business report," AI might generate something too generic to be useful. But if you provide more details, such as, "Write a one-page executive summary on recent trends in digital transformation for a corporate leadership meeting," you will get a much more relevant and targeted response. The difference lies not in the AI's capabilities, but in the clarity of your instructions.

Specificity also helps reduce inaccuracies. Imagine you're looking for market research on a specific industry. If you ask, "What are the latest trends in retail?" AI might provide a broad, unfocused answer covering everything from small businesses to multinational chains. But if you refine your prompt to, "What are the latest trends in e-commerce for mid-sized fashion retailers in North America?" AI will produce far more useful insights.

Clarity and specificity are even more important in the context of image-generation AIs such as Midjourney or video-generation such as Sora, where specificity can dramatically change the output. For example, crafting highly specific prompts that include intricate details—such as "a Victorian-era gentleman in a misty forest at dawn"—can result in more tailored and vivid outputs compared to vague instructions.

Context and Background

When interacting with AI, providing the right context is just as important as the question itself. Without proper background information, AI models may generate responses that are misleading or lack the depth needed for a useful answer. Just as a human consultant would struggle to give relevant advice without understanding the full context, AI requires well-structured input to deliver precise and meaningful responses. A prompt like, "What are the best strategies for customer retention?" will likely yield generic recommendations. However, adding context—such as your industry, target customers, and competitors—makes a significant difference. A prompt with more context like, "What are the best strategies for retaining customers in a traditional bank facing competition from aggressive fintechs?" will generate more tailored and actionable insights.

If you are unsure about how to structure your prompt, a good approach can be to ask the AI for a list of clarifying questions it needs to better understand context. For example, you could ask, "What questions should I answer to help you generate a more effective customer retention strategy for my company?" and the AI might respond with questions like, "What type of customers are you targeting?" or "What services does your bank currently offer?" or "What is your main competitive advantage?" By feeding your answers to AI, it will get a much better understanding of context.

It is important to note that while humans are able to understand context, AI is not very good at this, as shown by the Cornell University study "It Is Not About What You Say, It Is About How You Say It."[5] The study revealed that the way information is sequenced and emphasized can dramatically affect how LLMs process and understand that information. Their findings suggest that placing the context before the question improved the model's performance significantly—boosting accuracy by up to 31%. Even more striking, when certain parts of the input were emphasized—whether it was the context, the question, or both—accuracy improved by as much as 36%. The researchers noted that emphasizing the context generally had a stronger impact than emphasizing the question.

The Benefits of Good Prompting

The 2024 study "AI Literacy and Its Implications for Prompt Engineering Strategies"[6] highlights just how critical prompt-writing skills are when using AI tools. The researchers found that participants who crafted prompts with greater clarity—incorporating elements like specificity and context—consistently received higher-quality outputs from LLMs. In fact, prompt quality accounted for as much as 78% of the variation in output quality, reinforcing that better prompting leads to better AI-generated responses.

The opposite is also true. Vague, poorly structured prompts often lead to weak or irrelevant responses. Users then find themselves stuck in a loop—revising not just the AI's output, but also their own prompts, trying to steer the model more effectively. While some trial and error is natural, this back-and-forth quickly undermines the efficiency AI is supposed to offer. Paradoxically, rushing the prompting process to save time usually ends up costing more time. A poorly crafted prompt often requires multiple iterations, and in many cases, you'll spend more time correcting the output than if you had approached the task without AI at all.

On the other hand, investing effort upfront—thinking critically, adding detail, and setting clear parameters—pays off. The more thought you put into your prompt from the start, the more time and productivity you will save later.

While studies recognize prompting as a fundamental workforce skill, our survey reveals a significant gap between perceived importance of prompting and its use at work. Although 70% of respondents rated prompting as essential in the workplace, only 38% said their companies value it during recruitment and performance evaluations—highlighting a clear disconnect between expectations and actual emphasis on prompting.

But as AI systems evolve and become increasingly autonomous—capable of performing tasks without constant human input—a key question emerges: Will prompting become less relevant? On the contrary, prompting is evolving alongside AI, shifting from static instructions to a more strategic role—one focused on goal-setting, direction, and intent.

The Future of Prompting: From Questioning to Goal-Setting

Most traditional AI tools are reactive by design. They wait for human input—whether it's writing a poem, generating an image, or debugging a line of code—and respond based on the patterns they've learned.

But as we've seen, these systems don't truly grasp context or purpose. They execute instructions efficiently, but they don't anticipate, adapt, or act independently.

That's beginning to change. A new generation of AI—so-called AI *agents*—is emerging with the capacity to set goals, make decisions, and modify its behavior as situations evolve. If today's AI is a capable assistant awaiting direction, these new systems resemble proactive collaborators—agents that identify what needs to be done and initiate action on their own.

In this new paradigm, prompting evolves as well. It's no longer just about asking better questions—it's about setting meaningful direction. Prompting becomes a tool for defining objectives, establishing ethical boundaries, and aligning AI behavior with human values. We won't simply instruct machines; we'll guide them toward goals.

As the Greek poet Archilochus wrote, "We don't rise to the level of our expectations; we fall to the level of our training." The same holds true for AI: No matter how autonomous these systems are, they are only as effective as the frameworks we design for them. And those frameworks still rely on prompts—multi-step, layered, and strategic inputs that shape how AI acts, adapts, and decides.

This is why prompting is not disappearing—it's becoming more vital, more complex, and more central to leadership in the age of AI. Those who can structure these interactions—who know how to guide not just tasks but also thinking—will define the next wave of innovation.

By now, it's clear that prompting is an essential technical skill for making the most of AI tools. But prompting goes beyond machines— it's also about asking better questions of humans.

Prompting with "Beautiful" Questions

No question proves that good questions can have a transformative impact than the following one, which changed the trajectory of the aerospace industry:

What if rockets could land?

Years ago, this question sounded naïve—even absurd—to seasoned aerospace engineers and executives. After all, for decades, the biggest bottleneck in space travel wasn't just the cost of building rockets but the fact that each rocket was single-use: without the ability to land and be reused, every space mission required constructing an entirely new rocket and launch infrastructure, making space exploration prohibitively expensive. This limitation created a major barrier to increasing the frequency of space missions and to expanding to private space exploration.

SpaceX, the advanced rockets and spacecraft company founded in 2002 to revolutionize space technology and make space travel more affordable and accessible, was determined to break this cycle and make space travel commercially viable. To do so, it had three main options:

1. Source cheaper rockets from countries like Russia or China, allowing for a larger fleet at a lower cost.
2. Incrementally optimize SpaceX's operations, improving efficiency to reduce production expenses.
3. Rethink rocket engineering entirely, developing a groundbreaking landing system that would make rockets reusable.

The first two approaches were logical, incremental solutions—the kind that traditional industry leaders might have pursued. But by asking itself whether rockets could actually land, SpaceX chose the third option, asking a question that seemed unrealistic but contained the key to transforming an entire industry.

The result? In December 2015, SpaceX successfully landed the first stage of its Falcon 9 rocket in Cape Canaveral, Florida—a historic moment that paved the way for reusable rockets, drastically cutting launch costs and reshaping the future of space exploration. More than a decade later, SpaceX continues to refine and expand this technology through the Starship system—a fully reusable launch vehicle composed of two stages: the Super Heavy booster and the Starship spacecraft, designed to carry both crew and cargo to Earth orbit, the Moon, and eventually even Mars. The company has achieved reusability for both components, pushing human spaceflight further than ever before.

The lesson here is simple: it is questions—no matter how unconventional—and not answers, that unlock possibilities that others fail to see. "What if rockets could land?" was a question that challenged long-standing industry assumptions, and in doing so, redefined what was possible. In an era where AI can provide infinite answers, our greatest skill will not be in knowing—it will be in questioning and provoking ourselves and others to think differently.

In *The Book of Beautiful Questions*,[7] "questionologist" Warren Berger explores this idea, offering a collection of thought-provoking questions designed to help people make better decisions, spark creativity, and enhance relationships and leadership skills. According to Berger, a "beautiful" question must be ambitious yet actionable, serve as a catalyst for change, and inspire curiosity and reflection. While questioning is a critical skill for business success, many organizational and psychological barriers get in the way, as highlighted in Francesca Gino's study, mentioned earlier. That's why fostering a culture of ongoing inquiry is essential: like a modern-day Socrates, we must champion environments where curiosity is encouraged, and the fear of questioning is dismantled—creating space for learning, innovation, and transformation.

Building a Culture of Questioning

Company culture is often seen as something intangible or hard to define but, in reality, it is far more concrete than we tend to believe. It's not about mission statements, core values, or motivational phrases plastered on office walls; it is, instead, the small, everyday actions that define company culture. One of the clearest definitions of company culture comes from venture capitalist Ben Horowitz, who said, "Culture is what people do when you're not watching."[8] In other words, culture is shaped by the unwritten norms and shared understandings that guide behavior across the organization.

As the power of questions becomes increasingly important in the age of AI, company culture must evolve to embrace inquiry. That means fostering an environment where teams are encouraged to improve their prompting skills, not penalized for it. In too many workplaces today, using AI tools is still seen as "cheating," and asking questions can be interpreted as a sign of ignorance or inefficiency. But in reality, questioning is a superpower: It's how individuals unlock creativity, challenge assumptions, and ultimately, reinvent entire businesses and industries.

One leader who embodies this mindset is Dirk Van de Put, CEO of Mondelēz International. He actively promotes a "culture of questioning" across the organization—encouraging employees at all levels to challenge assumptions, reframe problems, and propose bold ideas. In interviews, Van de Put has emphasized that curiosity is not just welcome at Mondelēz; it's essential. He believes that in a world of constant change, asking the right questions is far more valuable than relying solely on past expertise. Under his leadership, the company has embraced agile decision-making, cross-functional collaboration, and rapid experimentation—practices that thrive only when teams feel psychologically safe to question the status quo.

Another leader is Satya Nadella, CEO of Microsoft, who famously shifted the company's culture from one of "know-it-alls" to "learn-it-alls"—a subtle but profound change rooted in encouraging employees to stay curious and humble. By promoting a growth mindset and rewarding those who ask better questions, not just those who defend their expertise, Nadella helped transform Microsoft into one of the most innovative and valuable companies in the world, as well as a leader in the AI revolution—and he did so not by dismissing seemingly "dumb" questions, but by actively promoting them.

The Power of Thought Experiments

A very powerful method for generating these kinds of transformative questions is through the use of thought experiments. These hypothetical scenarios test a hypothesis, theory, or principle by exploring its potential consequences. Their use in business was popularized by innovative leaders like Tony Hsieh of Zappos. Often framed as questions—even seemingly unconventional ones—they ignite creative and strategic thinking. Examples include, "What would you do differently if you were starting your business today?" or "How is my customer using my product in unexpected ways?"

Thought experiments, by nature, do not seek definitive answers but rather provoke reflection; the purpose of these exercises is not to provide immediate solutions but rather to stimulate speculative thinking, challenge assumptions, and expand our perspective of the world. They push us out of our comfort zones and force us to confront questions without obvious answers.

After all, *Homo sapiens* is the only species capable of operating in two distinct domains: in the world of facts, where reality is analyzed through observation and empirical experience, and in the world of imagination, where hypothetical scenarios can be explored through abstract reasoning. A thought experiment starts with an assumption that does not need to be true—and is often deliberately false—to test a hypothesis or generate new insights.

Albert Einstein, one of the greatest minds in history, used thought experiments to solve fundamental problems in physics. At 16, he asked himself: "What would happen if I could travel alongside a beam of light?" and the ideas that stemmed from this reflection led to the formulation of the theory of special relativity.

Interestingly, at first glance, thought experiments may seem like absurd or nonsensical questions. But never underestimate the power of "stupid" ideas—many of them have been the starting point for some of the most revolutionary discoveries in history, as it was in the case of the Polaroid.

Thought experiments remind us that progress often begins not with certainty, but with curiosity—sometimes sparked by questions that seem naïve or even impossible. They have fueled breakthroughs in science, business, and philosophy not because they provide immediate answers, but because they stretch the imagination. In that spirit, the professionals who will shape the AI era won't be those who rush to solutions, but those who know how to ask the kinds of questions—both to AI tools and to other humans—that expand what's possible beyond what we already "know." Questions that unlock not only human creativity, but also AI's vast repertoire of knowledge and capabilities.

Just as Socrates's questions challenged the status quo in ancient Athens, and just as SpaceX dared to ask, "What if rockets could land?"—the future will belong to those bold enough to keep asking. In a world where AI holds infinite answers, success will not go to those who "know it all," but to those who "*ask* it all."

How to Put Prompting into Practice

- **Assign a Role Before Every AI Interaction**
  Practice specifying a role (e.g., "Act as a financial analyst," "Act as a historian") before giving any AI prompt. This sharpens the relevance and focus of the answer—echoing the "role assignment" principle described in the chapter.
- **Rework Vague Questions into Specific, Context-Rich Prompts**
  Take one vague prompt you might normally ask (e.g., "What's trending in tech?") and rewrite it by adding clear context (e.g., "Act as a startup founder. What are three key trends in AI for SaaS companies in Asia, specifically after 2024?").
- **Challenge Yourself to Add Constraints or Format Requirements**
  Regularly prompt AI by adding explicit constraints (like word limits, tone, or format) to practice the "clarity and specificity" component—for example, "Summarize this article in 3 bullet points for a C-level executive."
- **Run a Thought Experiment Weekly**
  Following the chapter's emphasis on thought experiments and beautiful questions, practice once a week by prompting AI (or colleagues) with provocative, boundary-pushing questions. Examples: "What if our business couldn't sell physical products anymore?" or "What assumptions are we making that no longer apply?"
- **Use AI to Help Form Better Questions**
  Train yourself to not only ask questions but also to prompt AI to improve your questioning. For instance, ask, "What three questions should I be asking to challenge my assumptions about [specific project or decision]?"

What Does AI Do Differently from Humans?

- **AI Has Answers; Humans Ask Questions**

  AI excels at retrieving, processing, and organizing vast amounts of information—it can provide answers faster and more comprehensively than any human.

  Humans, however, are defined by their ability to question— challenging assumptions, redefining problems, and framing entirely new inquiries that AI alone wouldn't generate.

- **AI Recognizes Patterns; Humans Reimagine Possibilities**

  AI is trained to identify existing patterns within data, optimizing based on past examples and statistical correlations.

  Humans, on the other hand, can break patterns, imagine alternate realities, and leap beyond the available data—asking "what if?" and "why not?" questions to explore uncharted paths.

- **AI Operates on Knowledge; Humans Operate on Meaning**

  AI processes information syntactically, generating outputs based on data and algorithms without true comprehension.

  Humans assign meaning, purpose, and emotional context to information—they don't just process knowledge; they interpret it through values, ethics, and lived experience.

3

Data Sensemaking

IMAGINE A 5,000-PIECE jigsaw puzzle of the beautiful Rio de Janeiro landscape, with the iconic Dois Irmãos mountain in the background. A stunning image—but a daunting challenge: As you sit before the scattered pieces, from where do you begin? What's your instinctive approach to making sense of the chaos spread across the table?

Surely, you'll rely on visual cues—colors, patterns, recognizable elements in the pieces. A blue piece might belong to the sky or sea, a face to another part of the image, and so on. It's a slow, trial-and-error process, guided by intuition, memory, and a bit of luck. While this approach is creative, engaging, and even fun, we have to admit that it is also incredibly inefficient. You make mistakes, misplace pieces, and spend lots of time searching for just the right fit, constrained by your cognitive limitations.

Now, consider how an AI system would tackle the same puzzle. Instead of relying on colors, visual patterns, or familiar imagery like humans do, the AI approaches the problem from a completely different angle—actually based on the edges and not on the content of the pieces. Rather than getting lost in the complexity of the image, it focuses on structural and mathematical patterns that are almost invisible to us.

For instance, instead of seeing a yellow piece and thinking, "This must belong to the sun," AI categorizes the piece purely by geometric properties—edge angles, connector depth, and statistical fit within the overall structure. It rapidly analyzes all 5,000 pieces at once, identifying patterns in seconds, and—even more impressively—compares each piece against hundreds of thousands of possible placements. Much faster than our slow, social puzzle-solving sessions with family and friends, right?

AI's superiority in solving puzzles has been proven in the real world. Jigsaw, an AI-powered robot built by YouTuber Mark Rober—who counts over 60 million subscribers—competed against one of the world's top human puzzle solvers, Tammy McLeod. An MIT alumna and Guinness World Record holder for completing a 250-piece Hasbro puzzle in just 9 minutes and 58.32 seconds, McLeod was no ordinary challenger, yet Jigsaw won.

But AI's superiority is limited not only to puzzles or to games such as Go and chess. It also extends to all forms of decision-making in fields where vast amounts of data enable learning, training, and optimization. Whether it's in medical imaging—where AI detects diseases faster and more accurately than doctors—or in predictive maintenance, where it prevents equipment failures before they happen, AI has consistently demonstrated its superiority. As these models continue to evolve, their accuracy improves. AI is now expanding into more complex, human-like tasks: recognizing emotions, interpreting nuanced language, and optimizing decisions in ways that challenge our very definition of intelligence.

Wherever data exists, AI's superiority is not just possible—it's inevitable.

But there's one important catch, highlighting a fundamental difference between humans and AI: unlike human decision-making, AI decision-making lacks true understanding. This catch is best illustrated by philosopher John Searle's Chinese Room thought experiment.

The Chinese Room Thought Experiment

Imagine a person locked in a room who doesn't speak or understand Chinese. Inside the room, they have a set of instruction manuals written in English, explaining exactly how to manipulate Chinese symbols based on specific input–output rules. Outside, a native Chinese speaker writes questions in Chinese and slides them under the door. The person inside follows the manuals, matching the symbols to craft a response, and slides it back out—without ever understanding what was asked or answered.

To the Chinese speaker outside, it seems like they're communicating with someone fluent in Chinese. But in reality, the person inside has no comprehension of the language: they're simply following a set of instructions.

In short, AI—like the person in the Chinese Room—processes information syntactically, as it shuffles symbols, identifies patterns, and applies computational logic with impressive efficiency, but it doesn't understand the meaning behind those symbols. Humans, on the other hand, process information semantically: although inefficiently, we interpret it, give it context, and connect it to a broader understanding of the world.

This distinction becomes crucial once AI delivers its output. In Chapter 2, we saw how prompting—crafting precise, strategic questions—is critical to unlocking AI's potential. But good questions alone aren't enough. AI can generate answers and surface data, but it can't explain what those answers mean, why they matter, or how they apply to your specific context.

That's where *data sensemaking* as a skill comes in. It's the human ability to go beyond the raw output—to interpret, contextualize, and translate insights into informed action. Without this step, AI's output risks becoming misleading, biased, and unreliable instead of providing valuable guidance, especially in a world of almost infinite data.

Data Overload and the "Rearview Mirror Effect"

Much like when we solve a puzzle, businesses today are flooded with fragmented data. The real challenge isn't just gathering the pieces— it's understanding how they fit together and what bigger picture they reveal. And here's where AI holds a key advantage: it tackles these puzzles far more efficiently than humans.

We have reached a point where the sheer volume of data has far outpaced human cognitive capacity to process it alone—and it's growing exponentially. More than 90% of all the data ever produced by humanity has been generated in just the past decade. By the end of 2025, global data creation is projected to hit an astonishing 181 zettabytes. To put that in perspective, that's equivalent to 6.89 billion years of continuous Netflix streaming in HD—surpassing the current age of the Earth and approaching the estimated age of the Universe. Not even the most dedicated binge-watcher could get through that much content—just as no human, as smart as they might be, is capable of "making sense" of the current volume of data alone.

A 2023 Oracle study[1] found that 86% of leaders feel overwhelmed by the sheer volume of data in their company, and 78% report being bombarded by more information from more sources than ever before. As a result, 86% admitted that data overload is complicating decision-making in both their personal and professional lives.

Imagine you're planning a weekend getaway to the beach, just a couple of hours from home. You load up the car, gather the whole family, buckle up, and even queue the perfect playlist for the drive. But then, as you shift into first gear, you decide to do something strange: you drive staring only at the rearview mirror, never looking through the windshield.

How far do you think you'd get? Not very. The chances of crashing are almost guaranteed. You might be moving forward, but your eyes are fixed on what's behind you—cautiously swerving, veering off course, and constantly one wrong move away from an accident.

Of course, you might think no one in their right mind would ever choose to drive this way. Yet most companies today resemble a driver fixated on the rearview mirror—analyzing profit-and-loss statements, balance sheets, year-over-year comparisons—all metrics reflecting the past, not anticipating the road ahead. Why does this happen? For two main reasons.

First, as mentioned earlier, humans aren't naturally wired to process large volumes of real-time data. Second, historical data is easier to work with because it's already been collected, cleaned, and stored. It's organized, structured, and ready for analysis. Real-time data, on the other hand, is messy and demanding: it requires continuous monitoring, advanced systems to capture it as events unfold, and significant computational power to interpret it instantly.

The consequence is that critical decisions are based on snapshots of what has already happened instead of what's about to happen, and the risk of this approach is substantial. Few examples illustrate this approach better than BlackBerry—a striking cautionary tale of how companies can be blindsided not by a lack of growth, but by fixating on the wrong signals.

The BlackBerry Blind Spot

Let's rewind to the late 2000s. At the time, BlackBerry wasn't just a successful company—it was a cultural icon. By 2006, BlackBerry commanded around 40% of the U.S. Smartphone market and nearly 20% globally, thanks to its signature physical keyboards and the BBM, a secure messaging system beloved by business professionals, governments, and celebrities alike. Inside the company, confidence was high.

Then, in 2007, Apple launched the iPhone—introducing the touchscreen interface and the App Store, with the promise of revolutionizing what Smartphones could do. Looking back now, we know that Apple delivered on that promise, helping it become the first company to surpass a $1 trillion market cap. In retrospect, it is tempering to assume that 2007 marked the beginning of the demise of the BlackBerry.

But it didn't—at least not immediately. BlackBerry's user base soared from 8 million in 2007 to an impressive 77 million by 2012—a nearly 10-fold increase in just five years. On paper, they appeared unstoppable. Internally, confident executives proudly reported strong quarterly results, convinced they were on the right trajectory. Yet beneath that surface growth, something far more dangerous was quietly unfolding.

What BlackBerry's leadership failed to notice was that the market itself was shifting beneath their feet: while their own numbers appeared strong, the overall Smartphone market was growing much faster—and the iPhone was leading that revolution. New consumers were flocking to Apple's touchscreen interface, seamless app ecosystem, and intuitive design. Meanwhile, BlackBerry clung to what had worked in the past, focusing on incremental improvements instead of reimagining their strategy.

BlackBerry's leadership made a critical mistake: they fixated on internal metrics—unit sales, active users, and quarterly revenue—without considering them in the context of the broader market shifts. By the time they recognized the true scale

(continued)

(*continued*)

of the change, it was too late: their market share, once commanding over 50%, had plummeted to less than 10% within just a few years, and in 2018 it amounted to less than 1%.

Customers migrated en masse to iPhones and Android devices, shifting both network effects and their loyalty toward these new platforms. BlackBerry's attempts to pivot, whether by launching touchscreen models or overhauling their operating system, came too late.

BlackBerry's downfall wasn't due to a lack of data—they had plenty. Their failure lay in their inability to make sense of it and extract meaningful insights that would help them make the right decisions. Yes, they were driving their "car" looking through the rearview mirror.

Slow and inaccurate human decision-making that results from the rearview mirror effect is one of the main problems affecting organizations globally. According to a Forrester study,[2] for every hour a product team spends on actual work, another 48 minutes are wasted simply waiting for decisions to be made. This equates to more than 3.5 hours of "wait time" in an average 8-hour workday—nearly half the day!

But the damage of poor decision-making goes far beyond wasted time. It leads to misallocated resources, stalled innovation, and missed market opportunities. Projects get delayed, investments rely on outdated or incomplete data, and teams grow disengaged due to a lack of clear direction. Worse still, when decisions are finally made, they're often clouded by cognitive biases, emotional reasoning, or gaps in information—resulting in strategic missteps and costly avoidable errors.

Transforming Raw Data into Forward-Looking Insights

So how can businesses shift their focus from simply having access to data to actually making sense of it—transforming scattered real-time data into forward-looking insights? And how can humans move away from routine data processing tasks, which have grown far beyond our cognitive capacity, and instead focus on higher-order, strategic decisions? That's exactly where AI comes in, as it processes vast amounts of data with unprecedented speed and precision, transforming raw data into actionable insights.

As seen in the Jigsaw example, AI excels at processing vast amounts of data to uncover patterns and make predictions—tasks that are often too complex for the cognitively constrained human brain to handle alone. But transforming those outputs into meaningful decisions still requires human judgment. That's where the skill of *data sensemaking* comes in: the ability to interpret and contextualize AI's inputs and outputs to make smarter decisions.

Before we use AI to process data and generate insights, we need to understand the inputs we are feeding it—because not all data is created equal.

There's an important distinction—often overlooked—between data, information, and insights. To illustrate the distinction, consider this string of GPS coordinates: 44°20'42"N, 8°32'48"E. Unless you've memorized every spot on the planet, these numbers mean almost nothing to you. They're a perfect example of raw data: unprocessed, context-free, and meaningless on their own. Data is like an uncut diamond in the digital age—valuable, but not immediately useful. While machines can process vast volumes of raw data, humans struggle to make sense of it without structure or context.

But once you input those coordinates into a tool like Google Maps, something magical happens: the raw data is transformed into information—a pin on the map marking Celle Ligure, the small village in Italy where I grew up. Information is what emerges when data is processed, organized, and given context, making it understandable and relevant.

But while information is useful, it's not enough to guide meaningful decisions. What we truly need are insights—the result of connecting information, identifying patterns, and giving them context. That's what actually drives decision-making.

Neither raw data nor isolated facts lead to good decisions. Knowing that a set of GPS coordinates points to Celle Ligure doesn't tell me how to get there—whether I should take a plane or a train, where the nearest ATM is, or which seafood restaurant is worth visiting (spoiler: it's La Lanterna). The real insights only emerge when information is combined, analyzed, and tied to specific questions or inputs we define—yes, the prompts! Insights are the most valuable output because they allow us to identify meaningful patterns and draw actionable conclusions. They help answer the critical questions: "Why?", "How?", and even "What should we expect next?"

It's the responsibility of leaders and organizations to prioritize which metrics truly matter and to spot the unique correlations that reveal actionable opportunities. Crucially, this is a uniquely human task, and its relevance varies from person to person. For example, knowing the distance to the nearest ATM might be useful for one individual, but irrelevant for someone who only uses credit cards. Similarly, identifying the best seafood restaurant offers no value to someone with a shellfish allergy.

The same principle applies in business: in a world overflowing with data, the ability to identify and focus on the right metrics is a decisive competitive advantage. After all, it's the *correlations* among these metrics that often generate the most valuable insights. That's where Key Performance Indicators come into play.

Key Performance Indicators

Key Performance Indicators (KPIs) are the specific metrics an organization chooses to monitor in order to track progress, evaluate performance, and guide strategic decisions. But not all KPIs are created equal: some provide only surface-level visibility, while others unlock deeper, more actionable insights.

The key is not just to select the right KPIs—but to design them when they don't yet exist. Effective KPIs go beyond describing what is happening; they help explain why it's happening and what actions to take next. In some cases, existing metrics will serve that purpose. In others, you may need to create new ones—combinations, ratios, or derived indicators that better reflect your specific business context or strategic goal. Once those KPIs are in place, AI can process the underlying data to identify patterns, trends, and predictions—turning raw input into meaningful guidance. Some best practices to design KPIs that drive insights include the following:

- **Look for non-obvious correlations.** The most valuable insights often emerge not from isolated metrics, but from unexpected relationships between them. Linking employee engagement scores to customer satisfaction, or connecting delivery times to return rates, can uncover levers that truly drive business performance. Be creative and play around with these correlations, as they move us from simply measuring to meaningfully making decisions.

- **Tie each KPI to a decision.** A good KPI should be a compass, not just a rear-view mirror. Before adopting any metric, ask, "What decision will this help me make?" If there's no clear answer, the KPI is likely decorative rather than strategic. Insightful metrics are those that guide real-world choices—about where to invest, what to adjust, or what to prioritize.

- **Focus on causes, not just symptoms.** Vanity metrics may look impressive, but they rarely inform action. Metrics like follower count or download numbers might track visibility, but they don't reveal what's working, or why. Instead, focus on KPIs that point to root causes: retention rate, cost per acquisition, or Net Promoter Score (NPS) are far better indicators of what's driving sustainable success.

- **Balance leading and lagging indicators.** To see the full picture, combine metrics that tell you *what happened* (lagging indicators like churn or quarterly revenue) with those that forecast *what's likely to happen* (leading indicators like customer behavior patterns, site engagement, or deal pipeline velocity). The real power lies in connecting the two—using foresight to shape outcomes.

How Tinder's KPIs Evolved—And What I Learned

During my five years leading Tinder in Latin America, I discovered that not all metrics are equally useful. I learned firsthand that the most valuable KPIs aren't the ones you inherit, but the ones you design.

Early on, I tracked daily stats like downloads, swipes, matches, and active users. I reviewed the dashboard each morning, expecting clarity. But I quickly realized that absolute figures and raw data didn't help me make better strategic decisions.

Eventually, I began analyzing trends—tracking week-over-week percentage changes. This data-turned-into-information helped a bit: if downloads dropped, I could shift marketing tactics. But I was still missing the *why*. I had transformed data into information, but one step was missing: I had no true insight.

To fill that gap, I started looking for deeper correlations—especially the non-obvious ones. One of the most powerful KPIs I developed was something I called the "degree of self-esteem." It measured how many matches a user received relative to the number of likes they gave. In Tinder's design, a "match" only happens when two people swipe right on each other.

I discovered that users who matched once every two likes felt better about their experience: they were more engaged, chatted more, and as a consequence, had higher retention rates. Those who matched once every ten likes often disengaged. That single metric—an insight buried deep in the data—helped us rethink marketing, UX, and investment priorities across different cities and age groups.

The lesson? Don't track what's just available to you; track what helps you understand *why* people behave the way they do.

When companies and leaders move beyond conventional KPIs by redefining what they measure—tailoring KPIs to uncover hidden patterns and forward-looking trends—they gain a competitive edge others miss. It's not about having more data; it's about asking different questions and designing metrics that reveal unique opportunities. But even the most innovative KPIs are only as good as the data behind them. If that data is flawed, the metrics become misleading—and the promise of smarter, AI-powered decision-making turns into an illusion.

That's why it's critical to understand what happens when AI is trained on poor data—and what we can actually do to prevent it.

Fixing Poor-Quality AI Training Data

To get the best outcomes from AI systems, as discussed in Chapter 2, strong prompting skills are essential—but they're not enough on their own. No matter how well we prompt AI, we can't blindly trust its outputs—just as we wouldn't unquestioningly trust human judgment.

We've already seen through examples like the jigsaw puzzle analogy and the Chinese Room Thought Experiment that AI doesn't *understand* meaning—it merely recognizes patterns. This distinction matters. Because AI lacks semantic comprehension, it can't truly "judge" the quality or implications of the data it processes. If the input is biased or incomplete, the output will inevitably reflect those same flaws.

Ultimately, AI's decision-making is only as good as the data it's trained on. Can we assume AI-driven decisions are always reliable? Absolutely not. The quality of the outcome depends not only on the algorithm itself but, more importantly, on the integrity, accuracy, and diversity of the data behind it. This vulnerability becomes especially clear when we examine four key limitations that undermine AI's reliability:

- **Bias in training data.** AI systems learn patterns based on the data they are fed. If the training data is skewed, imbalanced, or incomplete—whether due to historical inequalities, underrepresentation of certain groups, or narrow data sources—AI will inevitably absorb those biases. Worse yet, because AI operates at scale and with speed, it doesn't just replicate these biases; it can magnify them, applying them consistently and invisibly across countless decisions.
- **Generalization problems.** While AI excels at identifying patterns within its training data, it often struggles when confronted

with unfamiliar scenarios or novel contexts. Unlike humans, who can infer, adapt, and apply past knowledge flexibly across different situations, AI lacks this semantic flexibility, and it operates within the narrow boundaries of what it has "seen" before.

- **Lack of context.** One of AI's fundamental limitations is its inability to grasp the deeper "why" behind the decisions it makes. Humans naturally apply reasoning, intuition, and an understanding of broader context when evaluating information or making choices. We can weigh ethical considerations, long-term implications, and subtle social cues. AI, on the other hand, functions purely by recognizing statistical patterns in the data it has processed—without any intrinsic comprehension of meaning, purpose, or consequence.

- **Hallucinations.** These occur when an AI system—particularly LLMs like ChatGPT—generates information that is false, misleading, or nonsensical, but presents it with the same confidence and fluency as factual content. Hallucinations typically arise when the model attempts to fill in gaps beyond its training data, extrapolating based on patterns without access to verified information. This might happen if the model lacks sufficient context, is asked about obscure topics, or is required to "connect dots" that don't logically align. The risk is that the output *appears* coherent and credible, making it easy for users to mistake fabricated details for truth.

Consider these examples: A very traditional company deploys AI to screen job applicants for leadership roles. The result? The algorithm favors men—because it was trained on historical hiring data reflecting past biases against women. Similarly, an AI model tasked with identifying animals in photos repeatedly labels a husky as a wolf—not based on the animal itself, but because its training data associated wolves with snowy backgrounds, and the husky happened to be pictured in the snow.

Failing to critically assess AI-generated content can lead to serious consequences—chief among them, the rapid spread of misinformation. Unlike hallucinations, which are unintentional errors, misinformation is often deliberately crafted and widely shared. A now-famous example is the AI-generated image of Pope Francis in a white puffer jacket, which went viral despite being entirely fake. While harmless in itself, it underscores a deeper concern: the growing threat of deepfakes. With tools like Synthesia capable of producing highly realistic videos from minimal footage, the potential for fraud, manipulation, and misinformation has never been greater. In this environment, the ability to critically evaluate and distinguish fact from fabrication has never been more essential.

So how can we tackle data quality problems before they compromise AI decisions? Here are some practical steps to improve the reliability of AI outputs and fix the poor-quality AI training data issue:

- **Audit your data sources regularly.** Assess where your data is coming from. Is it current? Is it diverse? Does it represent the real world—or just a narrow slice of it?
- **Detect and correct bias early.** Review datasets to identify imbalances—especially in demographic, geographic, or behavioral variables. Don't just clean the data; question it.
- **Diversify your training sets.** Actively expand datasets to include underrepresented groups, edge cases, and alternative scenarios. More diversity leads to better generalization and fairer outcomes.
- **Establish human review loops.** Create checkpoints where humans review AI-generated outputs before key decisions are made. Critical thinking is your last line of defense against flawed logic or hallucinations.
- **Document assumptions and limitations.** Make it a habit to log the known gaps or limitations in your data and models. Transparency helps teams make better decisions and prevents overconfidence in flawed systems.

When we fix the underlying data issues, our KPIs become more reliable and serve as a stronger foundation for smarter decision-making. The end outcome? Businesses are able to use the power of AI and carefully designed KPIs to turn their businesses from reactive to predictive.

From Reactive to Predictive Decision-Making

Traditionally, businesses have relied on historical data—analyzing past performance to shape future strategies. Today, however, AI enables a shift from reactive decision-making, based on outdated reports, to predictive intelligence, where real-time insights drive forward-looking actions. This shift isn't just about having more data; it's about using AI to turn raw information into actionable foresight, empowering industries to anticipate customer behavior, market shifts, and emerging technologies.

By transforming scattered data points into patterns, predictions, and prescriptive actions, AI enables all industries—from agriculture to retail and beyond—to break free from the "rearview mirror effect" and to operate with greater efficiency, foresight, and intelligence. This marks a fundamental shift: moving from reactive decision-making to a predictive approach.

No sector better illustrates AI's potential to shift businesses from reactive to predictive than healthcare, and no use case is more compelling than the diagnosis of multiple sclerosis (MS), a chronic disease that affects the central nervous system.

MS is notoriously difficult to diagnose due to its varied and seemingly unrelated symptoms, along with the absence of a definitive test. Patients often visit different specialists—an orthopedist for walking difficulties or an ophthalmologist for visual issues like blurriness or double vision. Viewed in isolation, these symptoms are frequently misattributed to less serious conditions, leading to significant delays in diagnosis.

AI can bridge this gap by integrating data across disciplines, detecting hidden patterns, and predicting MS earlier than traditional methods. A 2023 study, "Innovations in Multiple Sclerosis Care: The Impact of Artificial Intelligence via Machine Learning on Clinical Research and Decision-Making,"[3] highlights how AI can analyze extensive datasets—from electronic health records to MRI scans—to identify subtle indicators of MS, ultimately speeding up diagnosis and improving treatment.

A team of researchers at University College London (UCL), led by Dr. Arman Eshaghi, has developed MS-PINPOINT—a suite of AI tools powered by a deep learning algorithm called MindGlide.[4] This technology is designed to forecast how multiple sclerosis symptoms may progress, when the disease is likely to worsen, and which treatments are most likely to be effective. By analyzing real-world hospital data and MRI scans, MindGlide clusters patients based on shared clinical and imaging characteristics, allowing clinicians to personalize treatment decisions with far greater precision—moving beyond the traditional trial-and-error approach. Remarkably, it delivers results in just 5–10 seconds per scan, dramatically reducing a task that once required expert neuroradiologists and could take weeks under the UK's NHS workload constraints.

Another standout healthcare example of predictive decision-making can be found in the Mayo Clinic, ranked first in CB Insights' 2024 Hospital AI Readiness Index.[5] The Mayo Clinic has integrated AI into over 100 clinical workflows—including predictive models that identify patients at high risk of ICU transfer up to 24 hours in advance, enabling earlier intervention and reducing complications. It has also developed AskMayoExpert, an AI-powered platform that delivers real-time clinical guidance to physicians at the point of care, improving both the speed and consistency of decision-making.

Overall, the growing influx of health data from patient wearables—such as smartwatches, fitness trackers, and connected health sensors—and electronic medical records, combined with AI's predictive capabilities, is driving a shift away from today's reactive "sick-care" model, where treatment begins only after symptoms appear. Instead, it's enabling a more proactive, value-based approach focused on preventing chronic conditions and improving long-term health outcomes.

Similar transformations are happening across many industries. As AI, IoT, and automation advance, nearly every industry is becoming "Smart"—not just "Smart Hospitals" but "Smart Homes," "Smart Factories," and even "Smart Education." In agriculture, "Smart Farms" leverage IoT, automation, and AI to optimize crop yields, minimize resource waste, and enhance sustainability. In these sectors and more, AI is driving greater efficiency, personalization, and sustainability.

But here's the catch: as we increasingly rely on AI to transform our businesses—from predictive tools to agentic systems capable of making autonomous decisions—we must resist the temptation to relinquish our role in critically evaluating their decisions and outputs. The more we delegate decision-making to machines, the more vital it becomes that we, as humans, remain active stewards of those decisions. Without thoughtful oversight of data quality, underlying assumptions, and potential biases, even the most advanced AI systems can produce misleading insights—leading to poor decisions, loss of trust, and unintended consequences.

That's where humans come in. While AI optimizes for efficiency, it is human judgment that ensures the quality of AI's output.

The Role of Humans in Critically Auditing AI's Output

For decades, education trained us to complete assignments efficiently—essentially, to do the homework. But in the age of AI, the "homework"—data analysis, routine tasks, even content creation—is increasingly handled by machines. The human role? As Po-Shen Loh, professor of Mathematics at Carnegie Mellon University and former national coach of the U.S. International Mathematical Olympiad team (2014–2023), put it: "People used to go to school to learn how to do homework. Today, everyone needs to learn how to correct and revise the homework."[6] The human role has shifted from doing the homework to being able to critically review it.

Our competitive advantage now lies in reviewing, critiquing, and improving the outputs of AI systems. It's about asking the following questions:

- **Is the AI output accurate?** Don't take AI-generated outputs at face value. Fact-check data points, names, statistics, and quotes using reliable sources. AI can fabricate ("hallucinate") information, misinterpret prompts, or reflect outdated knowledge.
- **Is the AI output in line with the context?** AI lacks situational awareness. It doesn't know what's happening in your organization, team, market, or audience unless you tell it. Ask whether the answer makes sense given the specific time, culture, goals, and circumstances you're operating in.

- **Is the AI output ethical?** AI can unintentionally reproduce harmful stereotypes, discriminatory logic, or misleading narratives embedded in training data. Reflect on whether the output aligns with your values and those of your stakeholders.
- **Is the training data of high quality?** Before trusting an AI model's output—especially one used within your company—it's essential to examine the foundation: the data the AI was trained on. Because AI doesn't "think" the way we do, it simply reflects patterns found in the data it's exposed to. If that data is flawed, incomplete, outdated, or biased, the outputs will inevitably inherit those flaws—no matter how impressive the model appears on the surface.

AI can make decisions quickly—but only humans can ensure they are the right ones, for the right context, based on the right data. Your edge is not in asking just the first question. It's in iterating through the second, third, and fourth—deeply and critically.

In decision-making, this skill becomes crucial. Data sensemaking is the equivalent of teaching ourselves—and our teams—not just to copy and paste AI's output or blindly trust it, but to evaluate AI-driven outputs critically, spotting bias, incomplete logic, or unintended consequences before they shape real-world outcomes.

Consequently, the interplay between prompting and data sensemaking is crucial. Prompting equips us to ask the right questions, steering AI (or others) toward relevant answers or insights. Data sensemaking, in turn, enables us to critically evaluate those answers or insights—ensuring they are unbiased, accurate, meaningful, and actionable.

As a result, the best decisions don't come from AI alone—nor from humans alone—but from the collaboration between the two. After all, we make thousands of decisions everyday—some life-changing, others barely noticeable. Some require careful analysis and logical reasoning, while others are guided by instinct or habit. Most fall somewhere in between, blending intuition with rational thought.

While some decisions are novel and demand careful consideration of multiple factors, most are routine. We choose what to eat for breakfast, which emails to answer first, or which route to take to work—often without much conscious thought. These everyday choices are shaped by habits, past experiences, and, increasingly, the digital tools we rely on.

As we have seen, AI has undeniably surpassed humans in the analytical and logical side of reasoning, making it an invaluable tool for data-driven decision-making. It can process vast amounts of information in seconds, uncover patterns that might take humans years to detect, and optimize decisions with remarkable precision and speed. However, despite these strengths, AI still falls short in critical areas that define human decision-making—particularly in analyzing context, recognizing data biases, and applying judgment shaped by experience and values.

This is why AI achieves its full potential when paired with human insight. In market research, for example, AI can sift through vast datasets and uncover emerging trends, but only human intuition can contextualize those patterns—grasping the cultural shifts and emotional drivers behind consumer behavior. Similarly, in writing, AI is capable of generating well-structured content, but it often lacks emotional depth, originality, and cultural nuance. It's human intervention that adds storytelling, adjusts tone, and ensures real-world relevance, transforming raw output into something truly meaningful.

The true strength of human decision-making lies in qualities that AI cannot replicate: intuition, experience, and the ability to navigate emotionally charged or uncertain situations. Humans incorporate elements that are difficult to quantify yet crucial in real-world decisions. Unlike AI, humans can adjust decisions based on shifting priorities, emotions, and unexpected circumstances. We rely not only on logic but also on creativity and intuition—skills especially valuable in novel or ambiguous situations. Ethical dilemmas, in particular, require more than optimization; they call for moral reasoning and a deep sense of responsibility—traits that remain uniquely human, as we will see in the Emotional Transformation section of the book.

In the end, the future won't belong to those who gather the most data—it will belong to those who know how to use AI to make the most "sense" out of it.

How to Put Data Sensemaking into Practice

- **Prioritize and Redefine KPIs Regularly**
  Instead of relying on default dashboards, practice critically selecting 2–3 key metrics for each project or decision. Ask: Which data points will actually reveal leading indicators, not just past performance?
- **Contextualize Any Data Point Before Acting**
  To prevent rearview mirror decision-making, every time you receive a report, pause, and question: What external factors (market shifts, competitor moves, consumer trends) might be influencing this data?
- **Correlate Non-obvious Metrics**
  Just as with the Tinder "user self-esteem" metric, experiment with finding unexpected relationships between different KPIs—forcing yourself to dig beyond surface-level metrics.
- **Critique AI Outputs**
  Whenever AI delivers an insight or recommendation, treat it as a first draft. Ask: Is there bias in the data? What assumptions is AI making? What key variable might it be missing? This habit keeps you in the driver's seat.
- **Apply the Rearview Mirror Test**
  Before making any significant decision, check whether you're using only historical data. Consciously ask: What forward-looking or real-time data could help me see what's coming, not just what's happened?

What Does AI Do Differently than Humans?

- **AI Processes All Data Equally; Humans Prioritize Which Data Matters**
  AI doesn't naturally distinguish between relevant and irrelevant data—it processes vast volumes indiscriminately.

  Humans excel at selecting which KPIs and data points truly matter, filtering noise, and focusing attention on what drives meaningful decisions.

- **AI Identifies Correlations; Humans Define Causation**
  AI is designed to find patterns and correlations in data—but it lacks true understanding of *why* those patterns exist.

  Humans are better at interpreting causality, questioning whether a correlation actually indicates a meaningful relationship or if external factors are influencing the data.

- **AI Optimizes for Efficiency; Humans Apply Ethics and Judgment**
  AI aims to optimize outcomes based on past data and predefined objectives, often purely logically.

  Humans inject ethical considerations, long-term thinking, and contextual judgment that AI overlooks—especially in ambiguous or high-stakes decisions.

4

Reperception

HAVE YOU EVER tried pouring water into a glass that's already full? It overflows. Nothing new can enter. No one with common sense would expect a different outcome.

And yet this is how most of us go through life—our minds crowded with assumptions, opinions, and certainties. The only way to truly make space for the new is to first *empty the cup*—and no story captures this better than this classic Buddhist parable:

> Centuries ago, a professor visited a Zen master, eager to learn the meaning of life. The master began pouring tea into the professor's cup, filling it to the brim. Yet, he continued pouring, letting the tea overflow onto the table. Unable to contain himself, the professor exclaimed, "Master, why do you keep pouring when the cup is already full?"
>
> The master replied calmly, "Like this cup, your mind is already full—full of your own opinions and assumptions. How can I show you the meaning of life unless you first empty your cup?"

This classic Zen parable illustrates perfectly an extremely important concept, namely the "beginner's mindset." The Buddhist monk Shunryu Suzuki once said, "If your mind is empty, it is ready for anything; it is open to anything. In the beginner's mind, there are many possibilities, but in the expert's mind, there are few." The beginner's mind, or *Shoshin*, is often described as a mental state free from assumptions and rigid beliefs—a clean slate open to embracing new possibilities.

71

Ironically, this centuries-old wisdom has never been more relevant than today: in a world of rapid AI transformation and technological disruption, expertise becomes outdated faster than ever. What truly sets individuals apart now is not clinging to what they know, but to their ability to release preconceptions and stay open to new ideas.

But to truly embrace new ideas and adapt, we also have to let go—to let go of our beliefs, past successes, and experiences; to let go of the certainty that what worked yesterday will work tomorrow; and to let go of the safety of routine and the comfort of old playbooks. This process of letting go and rethinking has become a very essential skill to thriving in the AI era: the skill of *reperception*, which allows us to let go, reframe, and shift our perspective—turning insights into novel ideas and real innovation.

Embracing New Ways of Thinking with AI

So far in this book, we have looked at how asking the right questions (prompting) and making sense of the answers (data sensemaking) are critical skills. But there's one extra, essential cognitive step we need to take: What do we do with the insights we gain? What do we do with the answers to well-crafted thought experiments? Too often, we cling to outdated beliefs or rigid frameworks, even in the face of new evidence.

Think of an investigator so convinced of a suspect's guilt that they dismiss new evidence—like DNA from someone else found at the crime scene a couple of days after the suspect's arrest. Or a doctor who sticks to the original prescription given to a patient, even when new test results clearly indicate that the original diagnosis was wrong. Or imagine a construction company discovering that the land beneath their half-built skyscraper is unstable, but continuing to build anyway, simply to avoid admitting that they had been wrong and not wanting to waste the efforts made so far.

It sounds absurd, doesn't it? That's because it is. These actions aren't just irrational—they can be unethical, dangerous, and even criminal. Yet in business and decision-making, people often fall into the same trap: clinging to outdated conclusions that have worked in the past instead of adjusting to new insights with the skill of reperception.

I first learned about reperception during a fireside chat I hosted at a Banco Bradesco Private Banking Family Forum—an event held by one of Brazil's largest banks. My guest was Matias Muchnick, a Chilean entrepreneur and the founder and CEO of NotCo, a food-tech startup that has been disrupting the plant-based food industry since 2015 through its bold use of AI. The company had raised $235 million in funding, with Jeff Bezos among its investors.

At the heart of NotCo's innovation is a proprietary AI algorithm named "Giuseppe," which analyzes thousands of plant-based ingredients to create alternatives to animal products like milk, meat, ice cream, and mayonnaise. These simulations are designed to closely mimic the taste and texture of traditional foods, and the most promising ones are further developed in the lab.

What fascinated me most was the role of "Giuseppe the AI" in this process. As a good Italian, I couldn't help but immediately ask about the origin of the algorithm's name. Matias explained that it was inspired by Giuseppe Arcimboldo, a sixteenth-century Italian artist renowned for painting portraits of people whose faces were composed of fruits, vegetables, and flowers. The AI system itself operates on a similarly creative principle: using molecular analysis, Giuseppe identifies plant-based ingredients capable of replicating the full sensory experience of animal-based foods—including their structure, elasticity, flavor, texture, and aroma. It then sifts through a database of 300,000 ingredients, proposing innovative combinations to recreate products like hamburgers, chicken meat, and milk. Giuseppe proved to be so effective that it soon expanded beyond NotCo, assisting other companies in their plant-based innovations, including Shake Shack, where NotCo's AI helped develop a plant-based custard in record time.

As I listened to Matias speak, one thought kept running through my mind: How is this even possible? I had never imagined that a company could simulate flavors through AI, let alone generate countless combinations that enabled NotCo to produce vegan milk using unexpected ingredients like pineapple and cauliflower. Through AI's near-infinite iterations, these possibilities were explored, tested, and validated—paving the way for product innovation cycles that are far faster and more cost-effective than those of conventional food companies. What struck me wasn't just the technology itself—it was the mindset shift behind it. NotCo's team was practicing what I later realized was reperception.

But why is reperception so important? What I realized in my conversation with Matias Muchnick—and with many other leaders, entrepreneurs, and experts in the years that followed—is that in the world of AI, the boundary between the impossible and the possible is constantly shifting, and that what once seemed unimaginable is now just another problem waiting for the right AI algorithm to solve.

Making the Impossible Possible at an Exponential Rate

In 1965, Gordon Moore, a young engineer and co-founder of Intel, made a bold prediction: the number of transistors on a microchip would double approximately every two years, while the cost of computing would fall significantly. This insight—now famously known as *Moore's Law*—meant that computing power would grow exponentially, even as it became more affordable.

More than 60 years later, Moore's Law has proven remarkably accurate, shaping the evolution of computing and driving technological progress at an unprecedented pace—introducing exponential change across all business sectors.

But not all exponential growth is created equal—and today, we're facing the steepest, most disruptive wave yet. Once-impossible feats are becoming reality, driven by the maturity of the AI triad explored in Chapter 1: computing power (hardware), data, and algorithms. Of these, computing power has seen the most dramatic shift—moving from traditional CPUs (Central Processing Units), which process one complex task at a time, to GPUs (Graphics Processing Units), which can handle thousands of smaller tasks in parallel.

Think of CPUs as expert managers—efficient at tackling one job after another. GPUs, on the other hand, are like factory floors filled with specialized workers, each executing tasks at high speed. This parallel processing makes GPUs perfectly suited for the scale and complexity of AI.

At the forefront of this shift is NVIDIA, led by CEO Jensen Huang. NVIDIA has pushed GPU performance to levels that far exceed the traditional expectations set by Moore's Law. As GPUs began outpac-ing CPUs in performance growth, NVIDIA coined a new benchmark: *Huang's Law*, which observes that GPU performance is now improving at more than three times the rate Moore predicted—not just doubling every two years, but doing so with unprecedented speed and scale.

AI adoption is following the same accelerating pattern. If we look at how quickly major General Purpose Technologies have spread, the trend becomes obvious: while electricity took 46 years to reach 25% of the U.S. population, the Internet hit that same mark in just seven years.[1] AI then comes with an even more striking number: ChatGPT reached 100 million users in only two months.[2] While this is a global figure, it highlights just how rapidly new technologies are now being embraced—all contributing to an exponential world.

The hard truth is that companies that fail to adapt face an ever-growing risk of extinction. The average lifespan of businesses on the S&P 500 has plummeted—from 61 years in 1958 to less than 18 years by 2021. This sharp decline mirrors the relentless pace of disruption and turnover among market leaders. The trend shows no sign of slow-ing down: according to McKinsey,[3] by 2027, 75% of the companies currently listed on the S&P 500 will have disappeared—whether through mergers, acquisitions, or bankruptcy.

The big shift in business that made reperception necessary was the move from a linear to an exponential rate of change—across every sector, in every field. In the past, companies could afford to plan 3, 5, or even 10 years ahead with a reasonable expectation that the business environment, customer needs, and competitive land-scape would evolve at a steady, manageable pace, and that success often came from optimizing existing processes and following well-established playbooks.

But today the linear world is gone. Welcome to the era of AI, where the shelf life of our decisions, beliefs, knowledge, and ideas is shrinking faster than ever.

Change now is exponential, and the pace keeps accelerating. Think about your industry—regardless of which one you're in—and you'll likely agree: it has changed more in the past 5 years than in the previous 20, and surely, it will evolve even more dramatically over the next two to three years than it ever has before.

From self-driving cars navigating city streets to AI passing the Bar Exam, from autonomous drones revolutionizing package delivery to image generators creating hyper-realistic portraits of fashion models that don't exist, AI has transformed what was once deemed impossible into reality across countless industries.

Consider how SpaceX has achieved precision rocket landings—something once dismissed as science fiction in the aerospace industry—or how DeepMind's AlphaFold cracked the complex challenge of protein folding, accelerating medical breakthroughs. Of course, humanity has witnessed many breakthroughs in the past, but the real difference today lies not only in the rate of change, but also in its depth—namely, in the intensity and far-reaching consequences of each breakthrough.

Earth-2: A Digital Twin of the Planet

Would you believe it's now possible to create a digital version of the Earth—and even predict weather patterns down to just a few meters? It sounds like science fiction, but it's real. Meet Earth-2, a groundbreaking project developed by NVIDIA that created a digital twin of our planet. By combining AI, advanced simulations, and realistic computer graphics, it's changing the way we understand and forecast weather and climate. At the heart of Earth-2 is an AI model called CoreDiff, which quickly and accurately simulates weather conditions. It can zoom in from a broad, 25-km view all the way down to a sharp, 2-km resolution—something that was previously unthinkable—and it does all that about 1,000 times faster and with far less energy than conventional methods. This isn't just theory—it's already making an impact: in Taiwan, the Central Weather Administration used these AI models during Typhoon Gaemi in 2024, the strongest storm to hit the country in eight years. Thanks to Earth-2, they were able to predict the typhoon's direct path eight days before it made landfall—far earlier and more accurately than traditional forecasts.

All these breakthroughs highlight one thing: when the world changes exponentially, so must the way we think. We now live in an era where ideas, beliefs, and even entire industries have a short shelf life, and what differentiates the professionals who thrive isn't just their ability to make good decisions; it's their ability to continually update those decisions in the face of external change.

As technology advances at an ever-accelerating pace, businesses are feeling its exponential effects on multiple fronts: customer behaviors and expectations are evolving at unprecedented speeds, workplace dynamics are rapidly transforming, market conditions and business models are being upended, and competition is fiercer than ever. We, as human workers, entrepreneurs, and leaders, must open our eyes to this new reality. What once seemed unimaginable is now entirely achievable. More important, we must be the ones to shape and build that reality.

Reperception in Practice at John Deere

A great example of reperception in practice comes from one of the most traditional companies in the world: John Deere. Just as NotCo used AI to rethink food ingredients, John Deere used it to rethink their entire role in the market—evolving from simply selling farming equipment to providing intelligence and insights to farmers. After all, John Deere isn't just any company. It's the largest farm equipment manufacturer in the world, with roots dating back to 1837 when a blacksmith named John Deere developed the first commercially successful self-scouring steel plow. Since then, it has grown into an industrial giant, generating nearly $50 billion annually through its signature green tractors, lawnmowers, harvesters, tree cutters, and more. If something needs to be chopped, cut, mowed, sprayed, or moved, John Deere has a machine for it.

In 2022, I had the opportunity to deliver a keynote at John Deere's dealers' convention in Miami. Just before stepping

(continued)

(*continued*)

on stage, some leaders of the event pulled me aside and said, "Andrea, please don't describe us as an agricultural equipment company." I was surprised. "What do you mean? That's what you produce and sell," I replied. But they shook their heads and answered firmly, "No, we now see ourselves as a company that sells intelligence to the farmer." That moment stuck with me: John Deere had evolved far beyond manufacturing bright green and yellow tractors. Today, it operates as an AI-driven intelligence company, embedding sensors into its equipment and using advanced algorithms to help farmers optimize every aspect of their operations—from planting to harvesting—maximizing efficiency, yield, and sustainability.

John Deere even set a bold objective: to generate 10% of its revenue from software fees—a shift that not only boosts scalability but also increases profitability. By rethinking their role in the market and refusing to limit themselves to the traditional "scope of work" of an agricultural equipment company, they entered a space no direct competitor had touched. All thanks to reperception.

Recognizing and Breaking the Barriers to Reperception

As the term suggests, *reperception* goes beyond perception: it's not just about recognizing patterns, making decisions, or forming beliefs; it's about knowing when to let go of them. In an exponential world, thriving requires more than making the right choices—it demands the ability to abandon those choices when the circumstances around you shift. Yet more often than not, we do exactly the opposite.

Cognitive Traps That Stand in the Way of Reperception

Reperceiving is hard—there's no denying it. As humans, our brains are naturally wired to resist rethinking. We're programmed to think in straight lines, not exponential curves. Several cognitive traps make this even harder:

- **Confirmation bias.** We tend to filter information through our existing worldview, favoring facts that reinforce what we already believe and ignoring those that challenge us. In short, we look for validation—not disruption—of our assumptions.
- **Information bottleneck.** In today's world, we're bombarded with so much data that it becomes difficult to process clearly. Overwhelmed, we freeze, delay decisions, or default to what worked before—even when the context has changed.
- **Path dependence.** We often make decisions about the future based on what worked in the past. Familiar strategies feel safe, so we repeat them. But this comfort can blind us to emerging opportunities and new realities.
- **Ego reinforcement.** As we gain experience and rise in leadership, we may find ourselves surrounded by people who agree with us—validating our decisions, echoing our ideas, even laughing at our jokes. Over time, this can inflate our sense of being right and make it harder to challenge our own thinking, as noted in the Harvard Business Review article "Ego Is the Enemy of Good Leadership."[4]
- **The illusion of linearity.** Because we're wired to think in straight lines, one of the biggest challenges with exponential change is how deceptively slow it appears at first. Picture an exponential curve: in its early stages, progress seems gradual—almost flat. It creates a false sense of stability, leading many to believe they have time. But this illusion masks the urgency of change. By the time the curve reaches its inflection point—when growth suddenly accelerates—it can be too late to react. This illusion of linearity causes delays in decision-making, making individuals and organizations slow to adapt just when speed matters most.

How to Free Yourself from Cognitive Traps

While these cognitive traps work against our ability to reperceive, they affect everyone—creating a unique advantage for those who can break free from them. In this context, reperception becomes a powerful differentiator in the workplace. Professionals who are able to adapt their mindset, let go of old assumptions, and spot the curve before it steepens are the ones who gain a true competitive advantage. They're not only able to pivot and update their strategies; they can seize opportunities while others are still trying to catch up. To free yourself from cognitive traps and break the barriers to reperception, you should employ the following strategies:

- **Actively challenge your own assumptions.** Rather than seeking validation, make it a habit to ask: *What might I be wrong about?* or *What would someone with a completely different perspective see here?* This helps counter *confirmation bias* and opens space for new insights.
- **Simplify and prioritize information.** To avoid falling into the *information bottleneck*, develop systems to filter what matters most. Use frameworks, questions, or even AI tools to distill clarity from complexity instead of defaulting to old playbooks.
- **Question past successes.** Recognize when you're relying too heavily on what worked before. To combat *path dependence*, regularly ask: *Does this still serve us in today's context?* or *What would we do differently if we were starting from scratch?*
- **Create feedback loops that challenge your ego.** Surround yourself with people who feel safe enough to disagree with you. To break free from the grip of *ego reinforcement*, leaders must invite dissent, reward honest feedback, and model humility.
- **Build a sense of urgency before the curve steepens.** Train yourself to recognize early signals of exponential change and act before the inflection point hits. Overcoming the *illusion of linearity* means shifting from reactive to proactive thinking—anticipating disruption rather than waiting for proof.

We see reperception in action when companies challenge their assumptions and ask new questions about their role in the value chain. For instance, a domestic appliance brand reframes its identity—not just as a product maker, but as a data company—and begins using consumption insights to advise food manufacturers.

Others resist the pull of past success by rethinking their business models. A furniture company, for example, abandons the assumption that owning furniture is essential and launches a subscription service aimed at Gen Z—willing to disrupt its own core offering before someone else does.

We also see companies breaking the illusion of linearity and acting early on shifting trends. A car manufacturer anticipates the decline of traditional ownership and pivots to offering mobility-as-a-service, staying ahead of the curve while competitors are still anchored in the past.

In fact, many of the cognitive traps that block reperception— like confirmation bias, path dependence, and the illusion of linearity—are byproducts of the hyperspecialized mindset we've long considered the gold standard. When our identity and value are tied to deep expertise in a single domain, it becomes harder to let go of old frameworks, question past success, or remain open to radically different ways of thinking.

To thrive in an era of constant disruption and to practice reperception, we need more than specialization—we need cognitive flexibility.

Shifting from Hyperspecialization to Cognitive Flexibility

During the Industrial Revolution and much of the twentieth century, when knowledge was scarce, access to information was limited, and production systems were rigid, *hyperspecialization* became the dominant paradigm. The logic was simple: dividing labor into narrow, specialized tasks maximized efficiency, allowing industries to scale and workers to become experts in a tightly defined role. Success came from mastering a specific function within a predictable, stable environment.

But the world we inhabit today is vastly different. Information is no longer confined to a privileged few—it's widely accessible, often just a click away. Digital technologies and AI have democratized hard skills to such an extent that specialists no longer hold a monopoly on expertise.

As the complexity and unpredictability of our world accelerate, traditional job descriptions no longer reflect the reality of modern work. Roles today are fluid, interconnected, and made up of a wide range of evolving tasks—not just one or a handful of narrowly defined responsibilities, as was the case under the old paradigm of hyperspecialization.

For instance, kindergarten teachers perform 37 distinct tasks, while radiologic technologists handle around 30. Yet despite AI's growing capabilities, no job is fully automatable. These insights comes from Erik Brynjolfsson, director of the Stanford Digital Economy Lab, who analyzed U.S. Department of Labor data detailing the task composition of 950 professions[5] and confirmed that while AI performs exceptionally well on specific, narrowly defined tasks, it struggles to connect them in a cohesive, context-aware way.

In this new reality, humans lose their edge in hyperspecialization—because that's exactly where AI excels. What then becomes even more essential is *cognitive flexibility*: the ability to learn across disciplines, connect ideas, and apply knowledge in unfamiliar contexts. Success now depends on synthesizing insights from diverse fields and transforming them into meaningful and original ideas.

AI and machine learning have long demonstrated superhuman performance in narrow, well-defined tasks. Yet they historically fell short when it came to higher-order cognitive abilities—especially cognitive flexibility. Unlike humans, AI lacks the ability to transfer knowledge across contexts, reinterpret information in new ways, or adapt dynamically to unfamiliar situations.

François Chollet, former AI researcher at Google and founder of his own AI company Ndea, underscores this in an interview with Anil Ananthaswamy for *Nature*'s article "How Close Is AI to Human-Level Intelligence?"[6] Chollet explains that LLMs, no matter how advanced or large, struggle when faced with tasks that require recombining learned knowledge in novel ways. As he puts it, "LLMs cannot truly adapt to novelty because they have no ability to basically take their knowledge and then do a fairly sophisticated recombination of that knowledge on the fly to adapt to new context."

Consider an AI-powered chess engine: it can analyze millions of past games and predict the optimal moves based on established patterns, yet it cannot spontaneously invent a new strategy that falls outside its training data. A human, on the other hand, can sense shifting dynamics, break conventional rules, and redefine the game—just as

Magnus Carlsen did, pioneering entirely new styles of play. Take AlphaGo, for example. Although it famously defeated the world champion in the game of Go, its progress soon hit a ceiling. It couldn't refine its strategies independently, invent novel moves, or learn beyond the specific parameters it was trained on. Without human intervention or external updates, AlphaGo remained static—highlighting AI's limits in flexible, self-directed learning.

Similarly, an AI-assisted musician can compose music by drawing on patterns and structures it has learned, but it lacks the instinct to fuse different genres in unexpected, boundary-pushing ways. Take Miles Davis, for example: he didn't just follow familiar formulas; he revolutionized jazz by blending elements of rock, blues, and electronic music, creating entirely new sounds that no algorithm could have predicted.

AI as a Brainstorming Sparring Partner

But the fact that the ability to reperceive remains uniquely human, does not mean AI cannot help us develop and practice reperception. On the contrary, AI has become a tool to enhance it—pushing us to new cognitive heights through the generation of choices.

Imagine having an assistant for "out-of-the-box" thinking—an AI system not just designed to optimize existing decisions, but to surface novel, unexpected possibilities that might otherwise go unnoticed. The MIT study "Intelligent Choices Reshape Decision-Making and Productivity"[7] by Michael Schrage and David Kiron suggests that the ability to generate an immense number of choices in seconds is what makes AI so powerful in decision-making environments that need different points of view and reperception.

After all, choices are the foundation of effective decision-making, and without a diverse, high-quality set of options to evaluate, even the most sophisticated decision-making processes will fall short. Historically, organizations have relied on traditional dashboards and scorecards—tools built to track performance and ensure compliance, and while these are useful for monitoring progress, they were never designed to spark new insights, surface hidden opportunities, or challenge conventional assumptions. They show us what is, but rarely what could be. AI, on the other hand, can spark novel thought.

But while AI excels at generating novel outputs within predefined prompts or datasets, it lacks intentionality and contextual awareness. It doesn't choose which problems to solve, why a certain approach matters, or when it's time to abandon a creative path altogether.

Humans, on the other hand, bring uniquely human faculties that no dataset can fully capture. We can:

- **Define the problem:** framing the right question in the first place.
- **Set meaningful objectives:** aligning actions with goals, values, and long-term vision.
- **Evaluate trade-offs:** weighing risks, rewards, and unintended consequences.
- **Pivot with purpose:** knowing when to shift direction based on emotion, ethics, or strategic priorities.

These are not side notes—they are central to innovation, leadership, and decision-making in the age of AI.

In practice, when a team is brainstorming new product features, AI could introduce wildcard suggestions drawn from entirely different industries, sparking fresh cross-pollination of ideas that human teams might not have considered on their own. By expanding the range of possibilities, AI encourages curiosity, intellectual humility, and a broader perspective—all key ingredients of reperception.

However, there's a caveat. While AI has the potential to amplify reperception by generating diverse options, it can just as easily narrow it if we do not pay careful attention to its risks.

Recognizing AI Reperception Risks

One of the most significant risks that AI poses to our ability to reperceive is that of homogenized thinking: as more individuals and organizations rely on the same AI tools and models, their outputs tend to converge—making true originality and diversity of ideas harder to achieve. Generative AI operates within the boundaries of its training data, optimizing for existing patterns and prevailing trends, and while these tools can produce remarkable results, they also carry the risk of reinforcing what is already known, rather than pushing the boundaries of creativity.

The result? A landscape where outputs may appear novel on the surface, but beneath, they're variations of the same underlying structures. Instead of fueling breakthrough innovation, overreliance on AI may inadvertently lead to creative sameness.

AI systems, much like search engines, can also subtly shape our perception by prioritizing the most visible or popular sources in their outputs. Because these systems are trained on vast datasets reflecting dominant narratives, they risk reinforcing the same perspectives over and over. For example, when querying AI for strategies on "Digital Transformation," users across different countries might receive similar, mainstream responses—limiting exposure to diverse, local, or unconventional viewpoints.

Another significant challenge is the reinforcement of *echo chambers*. Generative AI models are trained on massive datasets that inherently reflect the biases, preferences, and worldviews of their creators and sources. As these models generate content, they often unintentionally amplify those existing biases instead of challenging them. This limits exposure to alternative viewpoints, trapping users in a feedback loop where their existing beliefs are not questioned, but rather, continuously reinforced.

AI-driven platforms, from YouTube to social media to search engines, personalize the content we see based on our preferences and behaviors. While this customization keeps us engaged, it also creates echo chambers that reinforce existing beliefs and limit exposure to diverse perspectives. As AI becomes more central to how we consume information, the risk of being trapped in self-reinforcing bubbles grows—making it essential to actively seek out alternative viewpoints rather than passively accepting curated content.

In the AI era, reperception isn't just valuable—it's essential. It's not enough to use AI tools passively; we must question their outputs, challenge their built-in assumptions, and deliberately think beyond the boundaries they set. Reperception allows us to break free from algorithmic patterns, uncover overlooked insights, and use AI as a springboard for real innovation.

While AI excels at recognizing and optimizing patterns, it lacks the distinctly human ability to redefine them. AI remains confined to its training data, unable to venture beyond it without human intervention. Human reasoning, by contrast, isn't limited to recombining existing information. It's about stepping outside known frameworks, using imagination and intuition to create entirely new ideas, not just to perceive, but to *reperceive*—constantly, deliberately, and with purpose.

How to Put Reperception into Practice

- **Redefine Your Own Scope of Work Regularly**
  Inspired by examples like John Deere and the developer who sees their job beyond coding, take time quarterly to rewrite your personal "job description" not by title or routine, but by the new ways you can add value—especially roles AI or technology might unlock.
- **Adopt a Beginner's Mindset**
  On a weekly basis, intentionally approach one problem, decision, or project as if you knew nothing about it—stripping away past expertise. Ask: What would someone without my assumptions or experience see differently here?
- **Identify One Belief to Let Go**
  Each month, reflect on a belief, strategy, or process that once worked but may no longer fit the exponential pace of change—whether it's a business model, customer approach, or personal habit—and consciously decide to "let it go."
- **Embark on a Cross-Disciplinary Learning Challenge**
  Dedicate time to learning from a completely unrelated field (e.g., a furniture brand studying SaaS models or an agriculture company studying data privacy). Practice connecting dots between disciplines.
- **Run a "What If We Weren't . . ." Scenario**
  Inspired by the John Deere anecdote, regularly ask provocative questions like, "What if we weren't a banking company but a data company?" or "What if we weren't a sales team but a customer experience team?" This forces mental shifts beyond fixed roles and industry boundaries.

What Does AI Do Differently than Humans?

- **AI Operates Within Patterns; Humans Break Patterns**
AI excels at recognizing and optimizing existing patterns based on historical data—it can remix and recombine information within the boundaries of its training set.
Humans, however, can question, discard, or reinterpret patterns entirely. We're capable of breaking out of old frameworks, letting go of past assumptions, and redefining the problem itself.

- **AI Lacks Intentionality; Humans Choose What to Reperceive**
AI doesn't choose which beliefs, models, or assumptions to challenge—it simply processes input as instructed.
Humans have the intentional capacity to decide when it's time to abandon outdated strategies or beliefs, consciously updating their mental models based on shifts in context or values.

- **AI Generalizes Knowledge; Humans Apply Cognitive Flexibility Across Domains**
AI transfers learning efficiently within narrow domains but struggles to creatively recombine knowledge from vastly different areas.
Humans leverage cognitive flexibility to connect dots across unrelated fields (like agriculture + software or food-tech + AI art), enabling true reperception and cross-pollination of ideas.

SECTION

II

Behavioral Transformation

5

Augmentation

IMAGINE WAKING UP every day to the same alarm, in the same bed, hearing the same song on the radio. You move through the motions—brushing your teeth, grabbing your usual coffee, driving the usual route to work. You see the same people at work, answer the same emails, sit through the same meetings. The day ends, and it feels like you've already lived it.

At first, it's frustrating. Then, numbing. Eventually, you stop noticing it altogether. You are stuck in a loop—performing, producing, executing—but never truly progressing.

In the 1993 classic *Groundhog Day*, Bill Murray plays a cynical weatherman who finds himself in that exact scenario: trapped in time, reliving the same day over and over again. The loop only begins to break when he stops going through the motions and starts reimagining what the day could be—not as something simply to endure. Nothing changes until he does.

It is a comedy, sure—but it also captures something deeply familiar: the soul-crushing weight of repetition. That feeling that we are busy, that we do a lot of things—not always the right ones and not the ones that elevate us—and that, deep down, we are stuck.

We get so used to this repetition that we do not even notice it. There is a deceptively simple question I often ask my MBA students, and now I ask you: "When was the last time you did something for the first time at work?" When was the last time you truly stepped away from your processes, habits, and routines and actually did something new? For most of us, the answer is, "It has been a while," because our workdays are dominated by repetition. Take a moment to reflect: How much of your day involves creativity, strategy, or learning something new, and how much of it is spent doing the same tasks you did yesterday?

Answering emails. Processing invoices. Updating spreadsheets. Generating reports. Logging data. In manufacturing, it might mean monitoring the same production metrics or running routine quality checks. In finance, reconciling transactions or approving expenses. In marketing, writing similar briefs or analyzing dashboards. No job, no department, no industry is immune to this.

Across industries and roles, people spend countless hours on tasks that are predictable, repetitive, and tightly woven into the machinery of business. According to Asana's *Anatomy of Work Global Index*,[1] 60% of working hours are taken up by this kind of "work about work"—the repetitive overhead of coordinating tasks, managing workflows, and tracking progress, rather than doing meaningful work itself—leaving only 26% for skills-based work and just 14% for forward-looking strategy.

It is no wonder, then, that a UiPath global survey[2] found 67% of office workers feel crushed by repetitive work—like a modern-day Sisyphus, condemned to push the same boulder up the hill each day, only to watch it roll back down again. Many long for something more: the chance to tackle meaningful problems, stretch their skills, or simply feel that they are building something that matters.

But let's be clear: these repetitive tasks do matter. Invoices must be processed. Data must be logged. Emails must be answered. They are the connective tissue of modern organizations—essential to keeping them running and profitable. The argument here is not that this work should stop being done. The argument is that it should stop being done by humans.

While these tasks are necessary, they rarely require what makes us uniquely valuable. Most do not call for creativity, empathy, strategic judgment, or ethical reasoning—at least not beyond the moment they are first designed or implemented. What they do require is consistency, speed, and precision—traits that AI now delivers better, faster, and at lower cost through task automation.

As discussed in Chapter 1, *automation* refers to the use of AI to handle repetitive, rule-based tasks—freeing us from the cognitive drain of activities that no longer require human input. It is a powerful solution to the "work about work" dilemma: instead of manually updating spreadsheets, chasing approvals, or sorting through inboxes, machines can now perform these functions better, faster, and more cost-effectively. But automation is only the beginning.

The true opportunity lies in *augmentation*—the use of AI not to perform human tasks on our behalf, but to amplify what we do best. Augmentation is a skill—an essential component of AI literacy—that enables us to use AI tools to maximize the quality, impact, and creativity of our human output.

What if we stopped seeing AI as a threat to our jobs and started seeing it as a powerful partner—one that helps us reclaim our time, energy, and attention? By automating what no longer requires our human input, we create the space—mentally and operationally—to focus on what still does, opening the door to more meaningful work. That is the promise of augmentation: using AI not just to automate tasks, but to amplify what humans do best—faster, smarter, and more creatively.

Automation may be the foundation, but augmentation is the differentiator. One clears the space; the other elevates the work. Together, they allow us to step out of the Groundhog Day loop and into a new paradigm of productivity—where our contributions feel not just useful, but uniquely human.

But to be clear, we can only enhance our uniquely human capabilities once the repetitive tasks have been automated first.

Automation: Paving the Way for Human-Centered Work

Before we can elevate the quality of our work, we need to first clear the repetitive, rule-based tasks that consume our mental bandwidth. Tackling automation head-on allows us to reclaim the time and cognitive space required for more creative, strategic, and high-impact contributions. According to Accenture's report *A New Era of Generative AI for Everyone,*[3] the potential here is massive: LLMs like ChatGPT could automate up to 31% of working hours in the United States—specifically tasks that require little to no human involvement.

However, the impact of automation varies widely across sectors. In industries like banking and insurance, where much of the work involves language-heavy, repetitive tasks—such as processing claims, reviewing loan applications, generating reports, the automation potential is much higher—54% and 48% of working hours, respectively.

In contrast, sectors such as life sciences and chemicals, which rely more on physical or hands-on work, show much lower automation potential—just 25% and 24%, respectively.

But automation does not stop at language. A wide range of non-language tasks—often more operational in nature—can also be automated through predictive AI, which uses structured data to recognize patterns, anticipate outcomes, and take action. These tasks range from simple processes like document classification to more complex operations such as inventory optimization or fraud detection.

Take Fortinet, for example—a global leader in cybersecurity. The company developed FortiAIOps, an AI-powered platform that automates and streamlines network operations by continuously gathering data from network devices, identifying anomalies, predicting potential issues, and proactively optimizing system performance. This is process automation in action: tasks that once required hours of manual troubleshooting are now handled automatically and in real time—freeing IT teams to focus on strategic work rather than firefighting.

In particular, three characteristics make a task especially ripe for automation:

- **Structure.** The task has clearly defined inputs and outputs, with repeatable steps that follow logical rules.
- **Familiarity.** There is a large volume of historical data or past examples that AI can learn from.
- **Low ambiguity.** Success and failure are easy to define, with little need for judgment, creativity, or contextual interpretation.

This list aligns with computer scientist Scott Aaronson's "Game Over Theory" discussed in Chapter 1: AI performs best when we have abundant examples of success and failure and where clear patterns can be learned. The more repetitive the task, the more suitable it is for automation. In many of these domains, AI does not just match us—it often outperforms us in speed and accuracy.

When it comes to speed, the impact of AI automation is nothing short of transformative. As NVIDIA's CEO Jensen Huang put it, "The majority of our chips are designed by Artificial Intelligence—without it, we would not innovate that fast."

This acceleration is not limited to tech companies. Take Dow Chemicals, for instance. By integrating predictive AI with Microsoft's tools, the company has reimagined its R&D process. What once took two to three months—discovering a new polyurethane formulation tailored to a specific customer—can now be achieved in just 30 seconds. That's a 200,000-fold acceleration in innovation.[4]

Speed is not the only advantage of AI. Accuracy is another. Take the example of self-driving cars. A recent study published in *Nature Communications*[5] compared over 2,100 autonomous vehicle accident reports in California with 35,000 incidents involving human-driven cars. After matching 548 comparable cases, researchers found that autonomous vehicles were, in most instances,[6] safer than human drivers.

AI's Productivity Paradox and the Commoditization of Execution

One might quickly conclude that the promise of AI automation leads to remarkable productivity gains and substantial value creation— by reducing costs and unlocking new revenue streams. Many experts share this view. According to McKinsey's optimistic report *The Economic Potential of Generative AI,*[7] the global economic impact could range between $2.6 and $4.4 trillion, driven largely by efficiency gains across the workforce.

But not everyone shares this optimism. Economist Daron Acemoglu, in his paper "The Simple Macroeconomics of AI,"[8] argues that AI's impact on total factor productivity—the gold standard for measuring economic efficiency—will likely remain below 1% over the next decade in the United States. His estimates suggest a cumulative gain of just 0.66%, largely because current AI applications tend to excel in routine, easily learnable tasks—the ones that generate relatively low economic value—while their impact on more complex, higher-value work will take much longer to materialize.

The first reason AI's impact may fall short of expectations is that, through automation, it is mostly making more efficient the kind of work that was unproductive to begin with. An article in *The Conversation*, entitled "ChatGPT: why it will probably remain just a tool that does inefficient work more efficiently,"[9] explores this challenge through the lens of anthropologist David Graeber's now-famous theory of "bullshit jobs." Graeber argued that many modern office roles are inherently unproductive, sustained by bureaucracy and internal process loops, and when AI automates tasks like formatting data, writing invoices, or compiling internal reports, it does not necessarily create real value—it merely accelerates processes that were already inefficient to begin with.

This disconnect—between technological promise and real-world productivity—is known in academia as the *Productivity Paradox*. It was explored in depth by Erik Brynjolfsson in his 1994 paper of the same name,[10] inspired by Robert Solow's now-famous line: "You can see the computer age everywhere, but in the productivity statistics."[11] That paradox is reaching new heights in today's AI era—and once again, it is being unpacked by thinkers like Acemoglu.

The second reason AI automation may fall short of delivering real economic gains is that its benefits quickly level out when everyone automates in similar ways. As the same AI tools become widely accessible, and every company automates faster and more efficiently, the competitive edge begins to disappear. Speed and efficiency stop being differentiators. They become the baseline, and in this scenario, execution turns into a commodity: no longer a strategic advantage, but simply the cost of staying in the game.

I experienced this firsthand—and if you create content on LinkedIn, you probably have too. In 2022, after some experimentation, I built an efficient AI-powered workflow to support my work as a keynote speaker. Each week, I wrote an article that ChatGPT translated into Portuguese and Spanish, adapted into Tweet format, and turned into a video script—all in seconds. What once took hours now took less than 10 minutes. I then recorded my podcasts and videos on Riverside.fm, used Magic Clips to edit and subtitle them in minutes, and created thumbnails in Canva. Even the article-writing process became faster, thanks to research tools like Perplexity.ai.

At first, it felt like a superpower, and I believed I would outpace competitors and stand out. But I was wrong. Scrolling through social media, I realized everyone was doing the same—posting high-quality content, more frequently. The same tools that had empowered me had empowered everyone else, and what once felt like a strategic edge had quickly become the new baseline.

This realization sparked a deeper reflection: In a world increasingly powered by AI, is execution still a differentiator? We previously explored how the abundance of knowledge led to the commoditization of ideas in our discussion of reperception. But once everyone had access to the same information, the true differentiator became execution—the ability to act on those ideas better and faster than others. This belief was crystallized in the 2002 book *Execution: The Discipline of Getting Things Done* by Larry Bossidy and Ram Charan,[12] which argued that success belongs not to those with the best ideas— but to those who can implement them faster and more efficiently.

Concepts like the First Mover Advantage became mainstream, and the idea that execution trumps ideation quickly turned into a business mantra. "Vision without execution is hallucination,"[13] Thomas Edison warned. "Ideas are a commodity. Execution is not,"[14] echoed Michael Dell. Even Herb Kelleher, co-founder of Southwest Airlines, captured it with typical bluntness: "We have a strategic plan. It's called 'doing things'."[15]

After all, even with the rise of digital tools and innovation frameworks, execution remained a formidable challenge—it was costly, complex, resource-intensive, and carried a high risk of failure. Ideation, by contrast, was relatively inexpensive and low-risk—often sparked by sudden flashes of insight, like Archimedes' legendary *eureka* moment in his bathtub.

This fundamental imbalance is what made execution so valuable: not everyone could do it well. The most successful companies and leaders were those who could execute faster, more efficiently, and with fewer mistakes—turning ideas into outcomes while others were still polishing their pitch decks.

But now, as AI accelerates familiar tasks, workflows, production, and delivery, execution itself is becoming a commodity. Simply building a product or launching a service is no longer a meaningful competitive advantage. AI is already speeding up execution across nearly every domain—from design and development to marketing, sales, and customer support. With the right guidance and input, AI can generate code, draft branding strategies, personalize communications, and even anticipate customer needs in real time, and this transformation is not limited to digital products alone. As AI begins to optimize and enhance manufacturing processes—especially when paired with widely accessible technologies like 3D printing and robotics—the acceleration of execution will extend into the physical world.

With each new wave of AI advancements—especially as models become more agentic, multimodal, and fine-tuned for specific industries—execution is becoming exponentially faster and more sophisticated. The question is no longer *if* AI will do it. The question is, "What is left for us to do?"

The consequence is clear—and challenging: in a world where execution becomes effortless, expectations will rise exponentially. Customers will no longer be impressed by functionality alone; they will demand continuous improvement, faster updates, seamless integration, and increasingly personalized, high-quality experiences. Therefore, end quality and human touch are increasingly valued by consumers in a world where execution is being commoditized by AI—and no company illustrates this better than Hermès.

As of 2025, Hermès was the fourth largest company in Europe by market capitalization, valued at approximately $300 billion. Its ethos was best captured by Creative Director Pierre-Alexis Dumas, a descendant of the company's founder, in an interview with CBS's *60 Minutes*.[16] The interviewer said to Dumas, "If I went to the Mercedes dealership and I said I would like that car, and they said, OK, you're going to have to wait five years—they'd be out of business." Dumas replied,

> You're talking about industrial production. You're applying your thinking structure of industrial production to craft. We're about craft. We're not machines. And we are not compromising on the quality of the way we make the bags. . . . [S]peed is the structuring value of the 20th century. We went from horse carriages to

the internet. Are we going to be so obsessed with speed and immediate satisfaction? Maybe not. Maybe there is another form of relation to the world which is linked to patience, to taking the time of making things right. You cannot compress time at one point without compromising on quality.

I know this might sound contradictory in a book that highlights the positive impact of AI-driven speed on business—but it is not. In fact, Dumas was reinforcing a central idea: that quality, which is amplified through augmentation, matters more than mere speed and efficiency, which come from task automation alone.

Hermès' strategy is deliberate: its most iconic product, the Birkin bag, is hard to buy—not due to limited capacity, but by design. Each bag is handcrafted by a single artisan over 20 hours, using carefully selected materials. There is no online store, no promotional push— just a waiting list. Scarcity, time, and craftsmanship have become part of the value. In a world where speed and scale are commoditized by automation, what stands out is what cannot be easily replicated—work infused with human care, meaning, and mastery.

Yes, the consumer's bar is higher now—and that is exactly why brands like Hermès, with their focus on quality and scarcity, and Italian shoemaker Golden Goose, with its emphasis on personalization and differentiation, are thriving. In an era where speed and scale are accessible to all, these brands succeed because they resist the pull of commoditization. They choose craftsmanship over mass production, uniqueness over uniformity—and in doing so, they stand out in a world increasingly defined by sameness.

In other words, as AI accelerates creation, it also raises the bar. That is precisely why the quality of our human work must rise in proportion to the speed that automation delivers.

So, what's the solution to AI's productivity paradox—and to the increasing commoditization of execution? It begins with recalibrating AI's role within our systems and organizations.

Returning to the insights of economist Daron Acemoglu—and to the central argument of this chapter—the answer becomes clear: we must move beyond automation and embrace augmentation too.

Augmentation: Enhancing Human Work's Quality

Daron Acemoglu argues that for AI to deliver real, sustained productivity growth, it must do more than automate routine tasks. It must amplify human capabilities—empowering people to tackle more complex problems, make smarter decisions, and take on higher-value work. In short, AI must augment us, not just replace us.

Instead of using AI solely to cut costs or reduce headcount, we need to focus on how it can elevate judgment, extend creativity, and amplify human potential. Because if execution alone is no longer a competitive advantage, then what is?

That is where augmentation comes in. Rather than replacing us, AI becomes a force multiplier. It is about using the time that automation gives back to us to improve the quality of our work—not just doing more, but doing better.

Before the Industrial Revolution, craftspeople built products by hand—each item unique, shaped by skill, patience, and care. Then came mechanized production, which did not eliminate craftsmanship—it complemented it: machines took over repetitive tasks, freeing artisans to focus on what they did best.

The same shift is happening now with AI. Like the machines of the past, AI can handle predictable, rules-based tasks. But it can also augment the creative process: designers using AI-powered tools to simulate and refine a new car concept are not being replaced—they are being empowered. Automation prioritizes speed and scale. Augmentation prioritizes human agency.

AI steps in as a powerful enabler of augmentation. In our daily lives, we already use AI-powered tools to enhance our capabilities: Grammarly and Quillbot to augment our writing (both among the top 10 most-used AI tools in the world in 2025[17]), Canva to augment our design skills, Perplexity.ai to augment our research, among many others. As Microsoft's Satya Nadella puts it, we are entering the "co-pilot age"[18] of AI, where the technology amplifies what we do best, rather than replacing us.

In business, a great example comes from Nubank, the largest digital bank in Latin America, valued at around $50 billion and ranked the third most innovative company in the world by Fast Company in 2025.[19] Early on, Nubank used AI primarily for automation: stream-lining customer service, managing transactions, and detecting fraud. It also built an AI Assistant powered by GPT-4o to handle customer inquiries directly, managing over 2 million chats per month and resolv-ing up to 50% of basic support requests—such as checking balances or resetting passwords—without human intervention. It handles up to five automated interactions before escalating, allowing human agents to focus on more complex cases.

But as the technology evolved, so did Nubank's strategy. Rather than replacing people, the company began investing in tools that augment employee capabilities—especially in areas where human judgment, empathy, and creativity still matter most. In partnership with OpenAI, Nubank developed a Call Center Copilot that assists agents in real time by integrating the bank's knowledge base and chat history. Built using GPT-4o, the copilot offers real-time multi-modal support—with next-reply suggestions, chat summarization, and step-by-step guidance. These solutions helped Nubank resolve queries 2.3 times faster, with higher accuracy, while maintaining a high customer satisfaction score (measured by Transactional Net Promoter Score, or tNPS, which gauges how likely a customer is to recommend the service after a single interaction).[20]

But Nubank is not alone. Around the world, the most forward-thinking companies are no longer just asking, "How can we automate more?" They are asking, "How can we build better human-in-the-loop systems?" The companies that win will not be the ones with the most automation—but those that strike the right balance with augmentation.

According to Accenture's *A New Era of Generative AI for Everyone* report, mentioned at the beginning of this chapter, 9% of working hours across industries, on average, involve tasks with high potential for augmentation—where AI supports human effort without replacing it. These are tasks that benefit from AI's speed and insight but still require human judgment, creativity, or decision-making.

As with automation, augmentation potential varies significantly by industry. The Accenture report breaks this down by sector: in Software & Platforms, for example, 21% of work hours are considered augmentable due to the high volume of technical and creative tasks.

Capital Markets and Insurance follow with 14% each—industries where AI can support complex analysis, risk modeling, and regulatory compliance, while still requiring human oversight. This zone—where AI assists rather than replaces—is where the greatest strategic value and potential for human–AI collaboration can be found, and organizations that learn to leverage it will be best positioned to lead the next wave of intelligent productivity.

Human–AI Synergy

A major study led by MIT Sloan professor Thomas W. Malone, "When Combinations of Humans and AI Are Useful,"[21] analyzed over 100 experiments on human–AI collaboration and found that while human–AI teams often outperformed humans working alone, they did not consistently outperform AI alone. In many cases, the combined performance was actually lower than that of the best individual performer—whether human or machine.

This contrast highlights two distinct forms of human–AI collaboration in execution. The first is human–AI augmentation—when a team of humans and AI performs better than a human alone, but not necessarily better than AI on its own. To go further, we aim for the second: human–AI synergy, where the combined efforts of both outperform what either could achieve individually. While augmentation is more common and easier to implement, true synergy remains a much harder goal to reach.

The hard part is determining when AI alone, humans alone, or a combination of both is the most effective approach. According to Michelle Vaccaro, an MIT doctoral student and co-author of the study, businesses frequently assume their AI is more reliable than it actually is, leading to inefficiencies in collaboration. But recognizing when to use AI is only half the challenge; the other half is applying that knowledge to real-world workflows. As Malone pointed out, effective AI integration isn't just about dividing subtasks between humans and AI; it's about redesigning the way they work together.

As AI becomes a more capable partner—able to take on an increasing share of our repetitive, structured, and data-driven tasks with speed and precision—we must evolve our role from task executors to curators of our own workflows. Our responsibility is now twofold: First, we need to identify the most repetitive and predictable parts of our daily routines—tasks that follow clear rules, require little contextual judgment, and reliably produce similar outputs—and learn to delegate them to AI. This includes activities like scheduling meetings, generating reports, organizing data, transcribing calls, and sending routine communications—in other words, the "work about work" defined earlier in this chapter: work that benefits most from increased speed and reduced error.

With the rise of agentic AI systems—capable of initiating and completing complex, multi-step processes—this delegation now extends to more dynamic workflows that span departments, platforms, and tools. Whether it's preparing a weekly KPI dashboard, drafting client onboarding materials, monitoring for system anomalies, or coordinating cross-functional updates, AI can—and increasingly should—handle the heavy lifting.

Second, we must protect and elevate the tasks that remain uniquely human. This means identifying the elements of our work that depend on empathy, critical thinking, ethical judgment, storytelling, creativity, and strategic vision and exploring how AI can augment these capabilities, not override them. Even when AI helps us surface insights, synthesize information, or generate creative options, it is still the human who brings meaning, direction, and purpose.

Doing this well requires more than smart delegation. It requires intentional workflow design. We need to develop the skill to choose when to collaborate with AI and when to act independently, to orchestrate hybrid systems in which AI is not just a tool, but a trusted partner. This demands a deep understanding not only of what AI can do, but of what humans do best.

In this emerging paradigm, our greatest competitive advantage is no longer our capacity to execute faster than machines. It's our ability to discern, design, and direct workflows where AI extends our potential, rather than flattens it. By knowing what to automate and what to amplify, we reclaim clarity, control, and purpose in a world accelerating toward complexity.

And this isn't just a theoretical ideal—it's already unfolding in practice. A white paper titled "Which Economic Tasks Are Performed with AI? Evidence from Millions of Claude Conversations,"[22] published by Anthropic, analyzed over 4 million real-world interactions with Claude, Anthropic's AI assistant. Using the U.S. Department of Labor's O*NET occupational database to classify tasks, the study found that 57% of usage reflected augmentation—AI supporting human effort—while 43% represented automation, with AI completing tasks with minimal human involvement.

These findings reinforce a powerful truth: the future of work isn't about choosing between humans and machines; it's about redesigning how they work together. And in that redesign lies our way out of the loop we've been trapped in—one task, one decision, one thoughtful collaboration at a time.

Like Bill Murray's character, we have spent years reliving the same professional routines—executing, performing, producing, but rarely evolving. AI gives us the opportunity to break free not by removing us from the equation, but by returning us to the work that matters most. Augmentation is about boosting the quality of human work in a world of accelerating automation and about choosing mastery over monotony—and just like in the movie, the loop finally breaks: not when the world changes, but when we do.

How to Put Augmentation into Practice

- **Audit Your Tasks Monthly**
  Set aside time each month to review your calendar and to-do lists. Identify which tasks share the characteristics of work ripe for automation—those that are structured, repetitive, familiar, and low in ambiguity. This gives you a clear picture of how much of your work could be delegated to AI.
- **Automate at Least One Task with AI**
  From the list of tasks identified, choose one each month and begin experimenting with AI tools to automate it. Start small, test, and refine—and gradually build your automation muscle.

- **Reinvest Time Earned into Higher-Value Work**
  Every time you automate a task, track the time saved.
  Then deliberately reinvest that time into strategic
  thinking, deep work, or creative problem-solving—
  instead of allowing it to be absorbed by more low-value
  or reactive tasks.
- **Augment a Human Workflow with AI as Co-Pilot**
  Choose a recurring process—like writing emails, generating reports, or conducting research—and redesign it with
  AI as a co-pilot. Define clear handoffs: let AI draft,
  organize, or analyze, while you focus on refining, judging,
  or deciding.
- **Elevate "Craftsmanship" into One Deliverable**
  Select one recurring deliverable and slow it down. Use AI
  not for speed, but to enhance craftsmanship, originality,
  or personalization—demonstrating that in an automated
  world, *quality is* your real competitive edge.

What Does AI Do Differently than Humans?

- **AI Scales Speed and Efficiency; Humans Scale Quality**
  AI accelerates execution, enabling rapid production and
  iteration—and does so with impressive accuracy.
  *Humans, in turn, elevate the craft—bringing depth, original-
  ity, and care that transform output into something memorable,
  valuable, and emotionally resonant.*
- **AI Automates Tasks; Humans Use AI to Augment Work**
  AI excels at handling repetitive, rules-based tasks.
  *Humans, by using AI as a co-pilot, amplify our capabilities,
  combining machine precision with human judgment to create
  smarter, more impactful outcomes.*

(*continued*)

(continued)

- **AI Depends on Humans; Humans Don't Depend on AI**
  AI, no matter how advanced, remains fundamentally
  dependent on humans—for training data, prompting,
  goal-setting, and oversight. Even agentic AI systems
  require direction and context.

  Humans, while at risk of overreliance, retain autonomy. We
  can choose when and how to use AI—or not at all. That
  choice is the ultimate source of our power.

6

Adaptability

CENTURIES AGO, IN a quiet village in feudal Japan, an old man named Takumi was taking his usual evening walk through the rice fields, when—gazing at the moon's reflection shimmering in the water—he suddenly realized his house keys were missing.

With the night already fallen and the fields cloaked in darkness, Takumi made his way toward the nearest source of light—a lantern beside a night watchman—and began searching under its warm glow. As he crouched, eyes scanning the ground, a young farmer named Hiroshi happened to pass by and paused, curious. "What are you looking for?" he asked. "My house keys," Takumi replied, without even looking up. "And where did you last see them?" Hiroshi inquired. Takumi pointed back toward the fields. "Somewhere over there." The farmer, confused, frowned. "Then why are you searching here?" and Takumi, puzzled by the question and speaking as if the answer were self-evident, replied, "Because the light is better here, and it's easier to search."

This Zen Buddhist story captures a deeply human truth: when faced with uncertainty, we often search for answers not where they truly are, but where it feels easier to look. We instinctively gravitate toward the familiar—toward what is lit, comfortable, and known—even when, more often than not, the real solution lies hidden in the shadows of the unfamiliar. As psychologist David Rock, author of *Your Brain at Work*, puts it, "Humans crave certainty and avoid uncertainty like it's pain."[1]

As humans, we have always wanted to believe that we can control our future—almost like modern-day Nostradamus figures or digital oracles of Delphi—and that with enough data, planning, and confidence, we can predict what lies ahead and shape it to our will. We convince ourselves that the decisions we make today, grounded in logic and information, are sufficient to guarantee the outcomes of tomorrow. But the truth is harder to accept: our sense of control has always been more illusion than reality. The belief that we can foresee and master the future isn't foresight—it is nothing more than *hubris*, a Greek term for arrogance, that blinds us to uncertainty, inflates our sense of capability, and places an outsized, and often misguided, faith in our tools.

Our need for predictability is hardwired into the brain. Certainty offers a sense of control and psychological safety, while uncertainty triggers a threat response deep within the limbic system. The more ambiguity we face, the more the brain treats it as danger—activating the amygdala, our internal alarm system, and pushing us into a state of heightened alert.

As a result, we become creatures of habit. In moments of uncertainty, our brains instinctively cling to the familiar—not because it's the most effective path, but because it feels safe. We fall back on mental shortcuts—heuristics—like "If it has always worked this way, why should we change?" or "If a customer asked for this, then it must be what they want," which help us act quickly, but not always wisely. And even when the familiar no longer serves us, we keep repeating it—simply because it's known.

The same pattern plays out in business. Far too often, we shy away from experimenting with new initiatives—not because they lack potential, but because they carry risk. We double down on short-term results, which feel easier to control—tangible, trackable, immediate—rather than investing in the long-term foundations our future truly depends on. We stick to familiar industries instead of exploring emerging ones, and we resist reinventing our business models for fear of cannibalizing existing revenue streams. But real innovation doesn't flourish under the streetlamp of certainty. It grows in the shadows, in the uncharted and uncomfortable spaces we tend to avoid.

In the previous chapter, we explored how AI can automate and augment the tasks we know best. But what happens when the rules no longer apply—when there's no training data to draw from, no historical precedent to lean on? That's exactly where this chapter begins: deep into the terrain of uncertainty.

Adaptability as a Key to Innovation

At the cognitive level, our ability to navigate the terrain of uncertainty begins with *reperception*—the capacity to reinterpret problems, challenge assumptions, and see familiar situations through entirely new lenses, as explored in Chapter 4. It's what helps us find clarity in the fog, revealing insights where others see only confusion. But insights alone aren't enough because, in the end, what's the value of a great idea that is not executed? Zero. To truly innovate and reinvent our businesses in the face of uncertainty, we need more than a new way of thinking—we need a new way of acting. We must test, build, and take ownership of outcomes we can't fully predict or control—and that's where adaptability comes in.

If reperception is about rethinking, then *adaptability* is about responding to change through action. It's the ability to adjust in real time, to take calculated risks, and to navigate uncertainty not just with fresh ideas, but with decisive movement. It's the leap from seeing differently to doing differently—the capacity to deliver in the present while simultaneously experimenting, boldly and intentionally, with the future.

The ability to adapt to change and navigate uncertainty becomes even more essential in a world that is, paradoxically, defined by uncertainty itself—accelerated by the exponential pace of change described by Huang's Law, that, as explored in Chapter 4, is overtaking Moore's Law in explaining the exponential acceleration of AI systems performance. As technological advances compound and market dynamics shift at breakneck speed, stability is no longer the norm; it's the exception. To thrive in this environment, we must learn not just to tolerate ambiguity, but to embrace it and to respond to change with the same velocity at which the world around us is evolving.

This presents us with a unique opportunity: while automation allows AI to free up some of our most valuable resources—like time, attention, and even courage—and augmentation enhances the quality of our work, what we gain back is the chance to focus on what is unfamiliar, unstructured, and unexplored. The more we delegate to AI what is known and predictable, the more space we create to venture into what is new, uncertain, and rich with possibility. In a world where AI increasingly outperforms us in familiar tasks, what remains distinctly and powerfully human is our ability to adapt to the unfamiliar.

Human Adaptability Versus AI Adaptability

The risk of not developing adaptability is anything but abstract—because it forces us to confront a critical question: What happens if we fail to respond to external change? The answer is simple: Someone else will. A competitor, a startup, or a more agile player will step in, solve the problem we chose to ignore, and take away from us the customer or market share we failed to protect. Disruption rarely comes from within—not because the problem was invisible, but because we were too anchored by habit, comfort, or heuristics to act on it.

Here's the paradox: even though we often resist change, we are still far better at responding to it than AI. Perhaps the simplest way to illustrate this uniquely human skill—our proficiency at adaptability—is with something I love almost as much as I love technology and that every good Italian like me holds dear: making a good cup of coffee.

The Coffee Test

Imagine the following: You are a Jiu-Jitsu addict like I am, and after a tough training session, a friend of yours heads home with intense back pain. It's a common enough situation in Jiu-Jitsu—you know he will be fine. The real problem arises the next morning, when he realizes he can't make his beloved cup of coffee. Since he lives alone—and martial arts create family-like bonds—you decide to show up at his door and offer to make it for him.

But because he can't join you in the kitchen, you're completely on your own.

At first, it seems like a simple task—after all, making coffee isn't exactly rocket science. But the moment you step into his kitchen, you realize it's more complicated than you expected. Where's the coffee maker? What kind does he use—a French press, a drip machine, or an espresso machine? How does it work? Does it take ground coffee or whole beans? Where are the filters? How much water should you use?

The real challenge isn't making coffee—it's performing a task you have mastered, but in an unfamiliar environment. In your own kitchen, you instinctively know where the mugs are, how your machine works, and what steps to follow. But in someone else's kitchen, you're forced to adapt in real time. There are no instructions, no familiar cues—so you rely on contextual intelligence: scanning the space, recognizing patterns, making educated guesses, and adjusting through trial and error. It's not about following a recipe—it's about navigating the unknown.

And yes, after some back and forth, a few wrong turns, and maybe a bit of frustration, you will eventually succeed. The coffee might not be perfect, but you will get it done.

Now imagine an AI-powered robot in the same situation. Could it do the same? Not yet. While making coffee may seem trivial, it is actually a deceptively complex task—which is precisely why it became the foundation of the *Coffee Test*, a benchmark for true Artificial General Intelligence proposed by Apple co-founder Steve Wozniak. The question is simple, yet revealing: Could an AI-powered robot walk into a random home, locate the kitchen, identify the necessary tools, navigate the space, and make a cup of coffee—without any prior instructions? The test is not really about coffee; it's about whether AI can understand, adapt, and act in unfamiliar environments the way we do.

AI's capabilities have long been put to the test. In the 1950s, British mathematician and computer science pioneer Alan Turing introduced what would become the first formal benchmark for artificial intelligence—the *Turing Test*—to evaluate an AI's ability to mimic human conversation.

The premise was simple, yet revolutionary. Turing proposed that if a machine could carry on a written conversation with a human judge—and do so convincingly enough that the judge couldn't reliably tell whether they were speaking to a human or a machine—then the AI could be considered intelligent.

While the Turing test focuses primarily on cognitive capabilities, the Coffee Test pushes the boundaries further. Just as adaptability goes beyond reperception—moving from thought to action—the Coffee Test shifts the challenge from language and logic to direct interaction with the physical world. It demands that AI engage in perception, motor coordination, real-time problem-solving, and—most important—adaptation in unfamiliar and unpredictable settings.

Why is the Coffee Test so difficult for AI to pass? Because even a task as seemingly simple as making coffee in an unfamiliar kitchen draws on a wide range of deeply human abilities—each one essential for functioning in the face of uncertainty:

- **Perception.** Perception goes far beyond identifying objects or reading labels. It involves distinguishing between similar-looking items—like sugar and salt, or a mug and a measuring cup.
- **Navigation.** In your own kitchen, you move without thinking. But in someone else's, you must explore and adjust in real time, making spatial decisions without a map.
- **Common sense reasoning.** You don't need an instruction manual to know that a coffee machine requires water or that a mug needs to be placed under the spout before pressing "brew."

These are skills we often take for granted—yet humans develop them over years of lived experience, trial, and error—and to this day, no AI-powered robot has successfully passed the Coffee Test.

AI may excel in structured environments—where rules are fixed, variables are known, and data is abundant—but it falters in the messy unpredictability of the real world. In practice, objects aren't always where they "should" be, machines differ in design, and even small errors demand on-the-spot adaptation. The challenge for AI isn't processing power—it's the absence of adaptive context. It can analyze patterns, but it doesn't *understand* them the way humans do.

When we compare how humans and AI differ in terms of adaptability, we can break the differences down across a few key dimensions:

Dimension	Humans	AI
Learning Approach	Observational and experiential	Data-driven
Flexibility	High in dynamic environments	Limited to programmed domains
Emotional Adaptation	Strong	Absent
Speed of Adaptation	Slower but more creative	Faster but constrained
Resistance to Change	Can resist due to habits	No resistance; purely functional

Despite its incredible advances, AI still struggles with key aspects of understanding and adapting to the real world. Below are some of AI's most critical limitations:

- **Lack of contextual understanding.** AI can detect patterns in data, but it doesn't truly grasp meaning. While it may recognize individual objects, it doesn't naturally understand how they relate to each other—or what they're for. It knows what things are, but not why they matter in a given situation.
- **No commonsense reasoning.** Humans rely on intuition and shared knowledge to make everyday decisions. AI, however, lacks common sense—the kind of background knowledge we take for granted, like knowing that water is wet or that you don't put a fork in a microwave. Without this, AI can make bizarre or illogical choices in unfamiliar situations.
- **Fragmented perception.** Unlike humans, AI doesn't integrate sensory inputs into a single, cohesive understanding of its

environment. It processes vision, sound, and text as separate streams, rather than combining them into a real-time model of the world. This leads to a rigid, incomplete perception of reality.

- **Inability to self-orient.** AI doesn't reassess or change direction on its own—it has no inner compass. Julian De Freitas, assistant professor at Harvard Business School and director of the Ethical Intelligence Lab, in his article "Self-Orienting in Humans and Machine Learning,"[2] explains that humans constantly update their internal understanding of where they are and what options they have as conditions shift. AI, on the other hand, lacks this adaptive, self-referential ability. AI systems can't "self-orient."

These limitations raise important questions about when it is truly safe to rely on AI—especially in unpredictable, high-stakes situations. Can an autonomous vehicle recognize that it's no longer navigating a road, but dealing with an entirely different challenge when it ends up in a ditch? Can a chatbot adapt its tone and response when speaking to a grieving family that has just lost a loved one? And how will AI perform when adaptability and not just automation becomes the decisive factor?

Because adaptability isn't just the passive ability to adjust to changing circumstances—it's an active, dynamic response. Like a scientist testing hypotheses and learning through iteration, we must be willing to pivot, refine, and rethink our direction as conditions evolve—even if that means letting go of what's currently working.

The Innovator's Dilemma

In 1876, Eli Lilly—a pharmaceutical chemist and former Union Army veteran—opened a modest pharmacy in Indianapolis. Above the door hung a simple sign: "Eli Lilly, Chemist." One of the first medicines he produced was quinine, used to treat malaria—a mosquito-borne illness that plagued much of the nineteenth-century world.

From those humble beginnings, Eli Lilly & Co. gradually evolved into a respected—though not dominant—player in the pharmaceutical industry. The company built its reputation on treatments for chronic illnesses, particularly in diabetes care, developing medications like Humalog and Trulicity that helped patients manage their symptoms over time. Lilly's strategy was steady and pragmatic, rooted in incremental improvements to existing therapies. Growth was consistent, but never transformative.

Until recently—when everything changed. The development of GLP-1 receptor agonists—particularly Mounjaro and Zepbound—catapulted Eli Lilly into an entirely new stratosphere. These drugs weren't just better treatments; they marked a leap forward in prevention, delivering dramatic improvements in weight loss and metabolic health. Suddenly, Lilly was no longer just managing chronic disease—it was on the path to potentially preventing it altogether.

The impact was staggering. By early 2025, Eli Lilly's market capitalization had soared to nearly $865 billion—the highest ever achieved by a pharmaceutical company—with its stock climbing more than 65% in just a year. In the third quarter of 2024 alone, Mounjaro and Zepbound accounted for 38% of the company's total revenue. Practically overnight, Lilly had gone from a steady legacy player to the most valuable pharma company in the world.

But with that meteoric rise came a paradox: What happens when your core business is treating diabetes—and you release a drug that may help prevent it entirely?

By preventing type 2 diabetes at scale, Eli Lilly's breakthrough could ultimately shrink the very market that sustained it for decades. In disrupting the future of diabetes, the company now faces a classic dilemma: its success today could cannibalize the demand for its traditional treatments tomorrow.

This tension is at the heart of what Harvard professor Clayton Christensen, in the 1990s, called the *Innovator's Dilemma*[3]—the paradox that companies face when confronting disruptive innovation. These breakthroughs often start as inferior, less profitable alternatives, which makes them difficult to justify within traditional business models. As a result, organizations tend to favor incremental improvements—safer, more predictable, and better aligned with short-term goals—over riskier, long-term bets. But that very hesitation can keep them from embracing the innovations that might ultimately define the future of their industries.

Eli Lilly's story brings us back to a fundamental question: What would have happened if the company had clung to its legacy business and ignored the shifting landscape—one where consumers increasingly prioritize prevention over treatment? What if it had chosen to protect its traditional revenue streams instead of disrupting them? Innovation often demands the boldness to undermine your own success before someone else does, and adaptability is precisely that—having the courage to pivot, even when it threatens the very foundation that brought you this far.

The paradox of adaptability is that it often runs counter to traditional business logic. By conventional metrics—like quarterly earnings, ROI, or market share—it can seem irrational to pivot, to invest in uncertainty, or to disrupt something that is already working. And yet the line between familiarity and uncertainty is the same line that separates short-term survival from long-term relevance.

Short-term goals are easier to manage—they come with clear metrics, immediate feedback loops, and a comforting sense of control. Success can be measured through quarterly earnings, customer retention rates, or operational efficiencies. The data is tangible, and the path forward is often well-defined.

As we explored in the previous chapter, these are exactly the kinds of environments where AI thrives—structured, stable, and rich in historical data. In such contexts, automation and augmentation generate immense value: optimizing processes, increasing speed and accuracy, driving down operational costs, and enhancing the quality of human work. It is no surprise, then, that AI's impact is strongest in the operational layers of a business—where short-term goals dominate and the focus is on what needs to get done today, this week, or this quarter.

The long term, however, brings an entirely different challenge. Metrics aren't just harder to track—they are often difficult to define in the first place, as we saw in our exploration of data sensemaking. Visibility fades, uncertainty increases, and outcomes become far less predictable. While we may optimize effectively for short-term wins, long-term impact is more elusive—harder to measure and even harder to control. For all its strengths, AI is poorly equipped to handle this kind of challenge—navigating the unfamiliar.

When the context is new, the terrain uncertain, and the rules still being written—when the focus shifts from immediate efficiencies to long-term strategic bets—AI begins to falter. Without a clear past to learn from, no historical patterns to model, and no reliable data to anchor its predictions, its strengths start to unravel in the face of the unknown.

Despite their growing sophistication, AI systems struggle with long-term planning. A study by Rao Kambhampati and his team at the University of Arizona[4] revealed that while OpenAI's o1 model performs well on tasks requiring up to 16 steps, its performance drops sharply when facing more complex scenarios involving 20 to 40 steps. This limitation highlights a central challenge in AI: while it handles short-term sequences with remarkable precision, it falters when asked to chart longer-term strategies—the very kind of thinking required in uncertain, evolving environments.

It's precisely in these moments that human leadership becomes indispensable. Balancing short-term execution with long-term innovation requires navigating some of the toughest trade-offs in business—not just because they're strategically complex, but because the real barriers are often psychological, financial, and deeply embedded in organizational culture. Among the most common barriers are the following:

- **The ROI problem.** You can't just easily measure what has not happened yet. One of the biggest barriers to long-term innovation is the difficulty in quantifying its value upfront. Unlike efficiency projects—where outcomes are clear, measurable, and often immediate—innovation brings uncertain, delayed, and diffuse returns. It's nearly impossible to predict when, or even if, a breakthrough idea will pay off—and in a world governed by quarterly targets and KPIs, the intangible nature of future value makes bold investments hard to justify. As a result, organizations tend to prioritize what is easily measured—even if it means underinvesting in what could be truly transformative.
- **Strategic cannibalization.** Sometimes you have to undermine what works today to build for the future, as true innovation often means competing with yourself. It requires launching

products or services that may disrupt—or even dismantle—your existing sources of revenue. This concept demands a bold shift in mindset: the willingness to weaken what is successful today in order to stay relevant tomorrow. It is one of the hardest choices a leader can make: to deliberately sacrifice what is working now in service of what could matter more in the future.

■ **Processes and routines.** Most organizations are built around processes and routines designed to optimize short-term performance—maximizing efficiency, minimizing errors, and delivering predictable results. But those same routines can quickly become barriers to adaptability. In rapidly changing environments, rigid processes often slow down decision-making and stifle innovation. What drives fast revenue today may ultimately limit a company's ability to respond to emerging challenges—and to seize the long-term opportunities waiting just beyond the familiar.

These barriers aren't just technical; they're deeply cultural. Embracing long-term innovation often requires companies to give up the comfort of predictable cash flows in favor of uncertain future growth, and it means accepting short-term revenue dips, navigating stakeholder resistance, and managing the internal friction that comes with breaking routines.

Nowhere is this dilemma more visible than in the impact AI is having across traditional industries. AI isn't just introducing new tools; it's redefining the pace of change itself. What once felt disruptive every few years is now happening continuously, and this new reality is forcing companies to confront deeper, more existential questions.

In healthcare, if illnesses can not only be diagnosed more accurately but also prevented earlier, what will the role of hospitals look like in the future? How will they make money? One possibility is that hospitals evolve into wellness hubs, focusing more on prevention, early intervention, and personalized health coaching. They may monetize continuous monitoring services using wearable and IoT data, offer AI-guided virtual care platforms, or partner with employers and insurers in value-based care models that reward health outcomes rather than procedures performed.

In the insurance industry, what happens when self-driving cars and AI-assisted driving lead to fewer accidents? Insurers may shift from traditional risk assessments based on historical accident rates to new models focused on cybersecurity threats, liability for AI-driven decisions, and coverage for system failures. They also may expand into proactive risk prevention services—using AI to deliver real-time driving insights, recommend predictive maintenance, and offer dynamic pricing based on vehicle usage and environmental conditions.

The most interesting part of all this? We don't have the exact answers. And perhaps more important—we're not supposed to. In a world increasingly shaped by complexity and unpredictability, the only way to find the path forward is through experimentation. We have to test, iterate, fail, learn, and try again—almost in a loop.

But here's the paradoxical upside: every time we experiment in uncertain environments, we're not just taking shots in the dark; we generate data.

More Data = More Adaptive AI

Every test, every prototype, every unexpected outcome becomes a valuable data point, and the more data we gather—especially from edge cases and ambiguous situations—the smarter our AI systems become.

This constant feedback loop creates a virtuous cycle: the more we venture into uncertainty and take intelligent risks, the more we strengthen the very systems designed to help us navigate it. In other words, uncertainty is no longer just a challenge; it's fuel. It's the raw material that powers the development of smarter, more adaptive AI—but only if we're bold enough to keep experimenting, even without guaranteed results.

A fascinating opportunity is emerging for traditional businesses. Historically, large organizations were seen as the most vulnerable to the Innovator's Dilemma. With significant revenue at stake, entrenched layers of bureaucracy, and a deep reliance on proven business models, these companies often struggled to pivot quickly or take bold risks. The opportunity cost of experimentation felt too high—and the fear of cannibalizing their own success, far too great.

In the age of AI, legacy companies are gaining an unexpected edge: data. Unlike startups still building their infrastructure, large organizations already sit on vast, proprietary datasets—accumulated through years of operations, customer interactions, and industry knowledge.

In this new landscape, data is no longer a byproduct—it's strategic capital to maximize adaptability. AI thrives on high-quality, diverse inputs, and traditional companies have the volume and depth to train models that anticipate change, detect patterns, and respond with precision.

Ironically, the very scale and complexity that once made these organizations slow are now their advantage. With the right mindset, they can turn legacy into leverage—experimenting intelligently, learning faster, and leading change rather than reacting to it.

Take Prudential, one of the largest life insurers in the world. In 2023, it announced a 10-year partnership with Vitality,[5] a leading health-monitoring app in Latin America. At first glance, the move seemed unexpected—why would a traditional insurance giant step into the world of mobile health and wellness? At first, I wondered if it was a case of losing strategic focus.

But after speaking with some Prudential executives at an event where I was invited to speak, the logic became clear—and deeply strategic. The reason? Data. Using smartphones and fitness trackers, Vitality users can engage in a variety of physical activities and track their progress in real time. What looks like a simple wellness app is, in reality, a powerful behavioral engine: it encourages healthier lifestyles while generating a steady stream of first-party data—capturing habits, routines, and real-world behaviors. Prudential can then use this data to personalize the insurance experience, gamify engagement, and deepen customer relationships. It boosts retention, builds loyalty, and turns passive policyholders into active participants. For Prudential's insurance customers, reaching higher Vitality status translates into tangible benefits—like annual discounts on their premiums. A win-win—driven by data and powered by adaptability.

This isn't just happening in insurance. At JPMorgan Chase, proprietary data has become a key asset in building AI models that outperform competitors in financial analysis and risk management.

While smaller players often rely on publicly available datasets, JPMorgan is leveraging its internal data infrastructure to develop models with greater depth, richer context, and higher predictive accuracy. In a world where open-source models are trained on shared data, proprietary data becomes the ultimate differentiator.

As AI regulation tightens and lawsuits—like the *New York Times*'s case against OpenAI and Microsoft, which accuses them of using millions of copyrighted articles without permission to train AI models—challenge the use of scraped content, the value of first-party data is set to rise dramatically. Companies that already own vast amounts of rich, clean, and well-structured data will be best positioned to win—not by sidestepping uncertainty, but by out-adapting everyone else.

Data isn't just something companies collect passively; it's something they can actively grow, even beyond their core business. Take Walmart, for example. In the United States, many Walmart stores have evolved into hubs for basic healthcare services—offering vaccines, blood tests, and routine check-ups alongside groceries and everyday essentials. At first glance, it might seem like a stretch: Is Walmart trying to become a healthcare provider? Or is this just a way to earn a small commission on added services?

Not quite. The real goal is far more strategic: to collect health data that can be used to personalize offerings, deepen customer engagement, and increase the frequency of meaningful touchpoints. With the help of AI, Walmart can turn that data into actionable insight—anticipating needs, customizing experiences, and enabling smarter, more adaptive interactions over time. In essence, businesses like Walmart are evolving into "one-stop shop platforms"—ecosystems where every service generates new data, and every data point enhances both decision-making and adaptability in equal measure.

But as essential as adaptability is in today's world, it is equally difficult to master. Let's be honest: navigating uncertainty is anything but easy. It's uncomfortable. It challenges our need for control, disrupts our routines, and pushes us beyond what feels familiar or safe—and that's precisely why, if we want to build real adaptability, we need to become comfortable in discomfort.

Being Comfortable in Discomfort

Think of something that gives you real pleasure. It could be anything—chocolate, music, a massage. Got it? For the sake of this example, let's go with chocolate—because honestly, who doesn't like it? Now picture this: you take a piece of your favorite chocolate, place it in your mouth, and let it melt slowly. That first bite? Pure delight. The second one—still great. Then a third, a fourth, maybe even a fifth. But by the sixth piece, something shifts. It's no longer as satisfying. You might even feel a little nauseous.

The same happens with music. Remember the hit *Despacito* by Luis Fonsi that caught the world by storm? Catchy the first time. Fun the second. But after hearing it on repeat in every café, Uber ride, and ringtone, it quickly went from addictive to unbearable.

As an economist, I can't help mentioning the Law of Diminishing Marginal Returns behind all this: the more we consume something, the less satisfaction we get from each additional dose.

This is also why pleasure can quickly turn into pain. In fact, researchers ran this exact chocolate experiment and found that after the fifth piece, participants began describing the experience as unpleasant. By the seventh, most said eating another would make them feel sick.

But here's the twist: just as pleasure can turn into pain, pain can also turn into pleasure, as both activate the same regions of the brain. While we have traditionally seen them as opposites, research tells a different story. In a compelling TED Talk entitled "Why We Need Pain to Feel Happiness,"[6] Brock Bastian, an Australian social psychologist, explores how discomfort isn't just something to avoid—it's essential to our capacity for joy. He points to the example of the "runner's high," the euphoric state long-distance runners often experience after an intense workout. By pushing our bodies to the limit, we unlock a surge of pleasure—ironically, through pain.

His argument is clear: if we endlessly chase pleasure, it begins to lose its meaning. But when pleasure is earned—when it follows struggle or adversity—it becomes more intense, more real.

To illustrate this, Bastian shared a fascinating experiment. Researchers first asked participants to describe significant adversities in their lives, resulting in a "lifetime adversity score." Then they asked participants to submerge their hand in a bucket of ice water for as long as possible. The findings were surprising. Those with little adversity removed their hand quickly—no surprise there. Those with a lot of adversity endured longer, which also makes sense. But the most intriguing insight came from those in the middle—people with a moderate level of adversity. Not only did they keep their hand submerged as long as anyone else, but they also reported the least amount of pain. They had developed the strongest resilience.

In a follow-up study, the same group reported the highest levels of happiness and well-being in life. The takeaway? A bit of pain—not too much, not none—seems to foster both resilience and happiness. What this tells us is that pain isn't just a signal of something wrong; it's a biological catalyst for change. Evolutionarily, discomfort drives action. Human beings who feel incomplete, restless, and unsatisfied are the ones most likely to seek solutions—and in doing so, to grow and innovate. Pain, in many ways, teaches us more effectively than instructions ever could.

Let's be honest: we don't grow inside our comfort zones. Real change begins in discomfort—when we step into the unknown and feel the friction of challenge. Unfortunately, more often than not, we resist that feeling. We treat discomfort like danger, even when it's exactly what drives growth.

Now, in the age of AI, this resistance becomes a serious liability. The world is shifting faster than ever—powered by exponential advances like Huang's Law, which predicts AI capabilities doubling every few months. In the analog era, you might reinvent yourself once or twice in a lifetime. Today, reinvention is continuous.

AI is pulling us out of our comfort zones—whether we're ready or not. Thriving in this world means getting comfortable with discomfort. Not avoiding it, but using it as fuel for transformation.

Great professionals in the digital age aren't the ones who avoid discomfort—they're the ones who learn to thrive in it. They adapt, experiment, and evolve not in spite of uncertainty, but thanks to it.

David Taylor, CEO of Procter & Gamble, often shares a story from his first day at the company's Cincinnati office. As he walked through the halls, a quote pinned to someone's cubicle caught his eye: "If I'm comfortable, then I'm part of the problem." The message resonated deeply. It became his personal and professional mantra from that day forward. It became mine too.

And today, it's the mantra of the most successful professionals in the age of AI. Because unlike Takumi, who got stuck searching under the beam of light, we must venture into the dark fields where the "lost keys" truly are—into the unknown where we will get lost, scared, or uncomfortable. And you know what? That's great. Because not only will we be driven to change and evolve, but we will also be collecting the data necessary to feed an increasingly adaptive AI—which, who knows, one day might just be able to make a cup of espresso as perfect as in Naples, Italy.

How to Put Adaptability into Practice

- **Map Out Your Innovator's Dilemmas**
  Identify areas in your work or industry where doing what's worked in the past might be holding you back from exploring what could work in the future. Ask: "Where am I prioritizing short-term efficiency over long-term reinvention?" Naming these dilemmas is the first step to navigating them consciously.
- **Design a Micro-experiment in Uncertainty**
  Each quarter, select one small initiative where outcomes are ambiguous or success is hard to measure. Timebox it (e.g., two weeks), run the experiment, and focus less on being right—and more on learning fast.
- **Collect and Refine the Data**
  After each experiment, analyze what happened—not just what worked, but why. Capture unexpected outcomes, edge cases, and moments of friction. These data points become the raw material for smarter decisions and better-designed systems.

- **Balance Short-Term Wins with Long-Term Bets**
  Inspired by Eli Lilly, set aside time, energy, or resources for high-upside projects with uncertain returns. Think of these as R&D for your adaptability: small risks today that build resilience and relevance for tomorrow.
- **Map Your Adaptability Triggers**
  Reflect on the conditions that help—or hinder—your ability to adapt. What gets you stuck? What helps you move forward? Identify patterns like perfectionism, decision fatigue, or lack of clarity, and design rituals or systems to support quicker, more confident action.

What Does AI Do Differently than Humans?

- **AI Performs Best in Predictable Environments; Humans Thrive in the Unfamiliar**
  AI excels when patterns are clear, rules are fixed, and historical data is abundant.
  Humans, by contrast, navigate ambiguity through intuition, experience, and context—even when no playbook exists.
- **AI Optimizes for the Short Term; Humans Pivot for the Long Term**
  AI is designed to maximize performance under current conditions, focusing on immediate outcomes.
  Humans, however, can zoom out—changing course entirely when needed and sacrificing short-term gains to ensure long-term relevance and resilience.
- **AI Processes Data; Humans Respond to Context**
  AI operates within predefined boundaries, often faltering when variables shift unexpectedly.
  Humans adapt in real time—adjusting goals, strategies, and behavior even amid sudden change or incomplete information.

7

Antifragility

On 26 April 2023, basketball fans around the world tuned in for a high-stakes NBA playoff game with massive championship implications. The 2022 NBA Champions Milwaukee Bucks were defending their title from the previous season against the Miami Heat in a crucial first-round playoffs matchup. Trailing 1–3 in the series, the Bucks were in a do-or-die situation—lose this game, and their season would be over.

The game was a rollercoaster of emotions, packed with dramatic twists and turns. The Bucks held a commanding 16-point lead in the fourth quarter, only to see it quickly slip away: with just half a second left in regular time, Miami's star Jimmy Butler hit a stunning buzzer-beater to send the game into overtime. In the final moments of overtime, while the Bucks had the ball, down 128–126, and as Grayson Allen drove toward the basket, time expired before he could get a shot off. Just like that, the Bucks lost—both the game and the series, 1–4. It was only the sixth time in NBA history that a No. 8 seed (Miami Heat) had eliminated a No. 1 seed (Milwaukee Bucks) in the first round of the playoffs. A crushing defeat.

If you're not a basketball fan, let me sum it up in one word: shock. The Bucks' early exit was so unexpected that I found myself watching the post-game press conference to see what their star player, Giannis Antetokounmpo, had to say about the defeat. He had played an incredible game, scoring 38 points and grabbing 20 rebounds. Yet despite his individual performance, his team had been eliminated.

I expected him to be devastated—and he was. But what unfolded at the press conference went far beyond frustration; it was wisdom. When a journalist asked Giannis whether he considered the season a failure, his response went viral—shared millions of times across social media—and for good reason. In my opinion, his words belong in business manuals and leadership courses, and his perspective on failure was so profound that it has stayed with me to this day. Visibly irritated, yet thoughtful and composed, Giannis took a deep breath and replied:

> Eric [Nehm, a reporter for *The Athletic*], you asked me this question last year. Let me ask you: Are you promoted at your job every year? Probably not, right? But does that mean your year at work was a failure? Every year you work toward a goal, like a promotion, to provide for your family and give them a better life, including taking care of your parents. All of that effort isn't failure; it's steps toward success. Think about this: Michael Jordan played professional basketball for 15 years and won six championships. Were the other nine years failures? Of course not. So why are you asking me this? There is no failure in sports. There are good days and bad days. Sometimes you win; sometimes you don't. That's part of sports—you can't win every time. Others are going to win too. Our goal is to get better every year. To build new habits, play better, and avoid bad stretches. We aim to win more championships. So, were the 50 years between 1971 and 2021 when we didn't win championships failures? No, they were steps along the way to the victory we finally achieved. We hope to win more in the future.[1]

Giannis's response gave me chills. It wasn't just a lesson in handling a basketball game loss—it was a masterclass in how to approach life. He didn't see failure as a dead end, but as a necessary step in the journey toward long-term success. This mindset isn't only powerful in sports; it's essential everywhere, from science to business, especially in the age of AI, where change and uncertainty are greater than ever.

But here's the paradox: the more we experiment in unfamiliar territory, the more we're bound to fail. That's the price of navigating uncertainty. And that brings us to the heart of this chapter: If failure is inevitable, we must learn to fail better, to fail smarter, to turn every setback into a stepping stone. Giannis's now-iconic response was a powerful reminder that in sports, as in life, failure is not the end—it's part of the path to success.

This mindset isn't unique to sports. In fact, the people who embrace it most consistently aren't athletes; they are scientists. Nowhere is this approach more vital than in scientific research, where mistakes aren't seen as failures, but as necessary steps on the path to discovery.

My Mother, the Scientist: A Lesson in Failing Forward

My mother has had a decades-long career as a cancer researcher at the University of Genova in Italy, where she also teaches Human Anatomy to aspiring doctors. From her, I learned the importance of making mistakes.

I still remember days as a teenager, waiting for my mom to come home from work. Some days, she would walk through the door with a smile, her excitement radiating across the room. Seeing her like that, I couldn't help but share in her enthusiasm, certain she had made a groundbreaking discovery—maybe even the kind that would make my dream of becoming the son of a Nobel Prize winner come true. Eager for the big news, I would rush to ask, "Mom, tell me! What did you discover?"

But instead of the exhilarating revelation I was expecting, she would give me a puzzled look and say, simply, that she hadn't discovered anything.

My teenage brain couldn't make sense of it. Like so many others, I had been conditioned to believe that success meant achieving something tangible—and that anything less was just failure by another name. If there was no discovery, how could it possibly have been a good day at work? That's what I would ask her, time and again.

Yet time and again, my mother's response challenged that mindset. She showed me that in science, failure isn't a

(continued)

(*continued*)

setback—it's essential. Her day had been great, not because she had discovered something new, but because she had run multiple experiments. And even though every one of them had "failed," each had revealed something valuable, bringing her one step closer to her next breakthrough. Yes, it wasn't the absence of failure that made her day a success—it was the act of learning itself, even (or especially) through failure.

Think of a scientist who does not allow themselves to fail. Will they ever discover anything? Of course not—they won't even start experimenting. In science, failure isn't the end; it's part of the process. My mother taught me that every failed experiment is a chance to learn, refine, and move one step closer to the truth. Scientists don't fear mistakes; they welcome them. Without failure, there is no discovery.

But here's the catch: sports and science are the exception, not the rule. In most other fields—business in particular—mistakes and failures are treated very differently. In fact, the mindset is often the exact opposite.

The Business World's Aversion to Failure

In the business world, mistakes are often treated as career-killers: employees hide their errors, leaders avoid risks, and innovation gets strangled by the fear of looking incompetent.

This aversion to failure breeds a culture of caution, where people hesitate to take risks or explore new ideas—worried about the consequences if things go wrong. The result is a cycle of conformity that stifles creativity, discourages collaboration, and ultimately holds the company back.

In environments with low tolerance for mistakes, failure isn't just avoided; it's swept under the rug. Transparency erodes, honest conversations disappear, and the organization loses the very qualities that drive progress. It is a true recipe for disaster.

But why is this the case? Why are mistakes at work treated like taboos—so undesirable that they are seen as threats to careers and reputations? Why do so many professionals hide their errors instead of reflecting on them and learning from the experience? And perhaps most troubling, why do organizations mostly reward those who play it safe, while overlooking the value of those who take bold risks, push boundaries, but occasionally stumble on the path to innovation?

Simply put, they fear the negative consequences. From financial loss and wasted time to emotional stress and reputational damage, mistakes carry a heavy cost, and in environments obsessed with short-term results, the instinct is to avoid errors at all costs—which often means avoiding experimentation altogether. In high-stakes fields like surgery and civil construction, the fear runs even deeper, as mistakes there can have life-or-death consequences.

The Upside of Mistakes: Antifragility

But what if we flipped the question? Instead of focusing on the negative consequences of mistakes, what if we asked: What can be their positive outcomes?

A bit trickier to answer, isn't it? Yet the upsides are real—and powerful. Here are the main ones:

- **Learning.** Mistakes reveal what went wrong and often uncover insights we might never discover under perfect conditions.
- **Collaboration.** Mistakes remind us that we are not perfect, encouraging us to ask for help and work more openly with others.
- **Sharper decision-making.** Failed attempts show us what doesn't work, helping us eliminate bad paths more quickly.
- **Real change and growth.** We often grow more from failure than from success because setbacks force us to pause, reflect, adapt, and evolve.

So what does all of this have to do with AI? Quite a lot. AI is a powerful tool for transforming how we deal with mistakes at work—minimizing their downsides, while amplifying their benefits. By using AI to learn faster from our failures and to reduce their costs, we ultimately turn mistakes into smart, strategic assets.

In 1889, the philosopher Friedrich Nietzsche wrote, "That which does not kill me makes me stronger" in *Twilight of the Idols*.[2] Over time, his words have become a staple of motivational speeches and internet memes, often used to promote resilience. But the ability to grow stronger through crises and mistakes goes beyond *resilience*—a word that comes from the Latin *resilire*, meaning "to return to a previous state." True growth isn't just about enduring hardship and bouncing back; it's about using mistakes and failures as catalysts for improvement, emerging stronger than before.

In 2012, economist and philosopher Nassim Nicholas Taleb introduced a term that perfectly captures this idea in his book *Antifragile: Things That Gain from Disorder*. The term is *antifragility*.[3] He defines it as the ability of systems to increase their capacity to thrive when exposed to stressors, shocks, volatility, noise, mistakes, failures, or even external attacks. Unlike fragile systems, which break under pressure, or resilient ones, which simply withstand it, antifragile systems evolve and grow stronger *because* of it.

For you to better understand the concept of antifragility, let me take you on a journey. A few years ago, I set out on a transformative solo trip through Asia, backpacking across Thailand, Laos, Vietnam, and Cambodia. After landing in Bangkok, I decided to shake off my 12-hour jet lag with a jiu-jitsu training session—a personal tradition whenever I visit a new place. As a black belt, I was eager not just to train but also to meet new people, and luckily, I found a gym near my hotel that offered both jiu-jitsu and Thai boxing, also known as Muay Thai.

While I felt completely at home on the jiu-jitsu mats, Muay Thai was still an unfamiliar art. As I trained, I found myself glancing at the local fighters, watching them refine their striking techniques with precision and focus.

One practice, in particular, caught my attention. Before stepping into the ring, the Muay Thai fighters rolled glass bottles up and down their shins with intense pressure, repeating the process for several minutes. Curious, I asked the trainer what they were doing. He explained that the technique deliberately causes microtrauma to the bone while desensitizing the nerves in the shin, ultimately making their legs stronger and more resistant to their opponents' leg kicks. Over time, the body responds to these repeated micro-injuries by reinforcing the bone structure and increasing pain tolerance. Yes, as counterintuitive as it sounds, bones actually become stronger after they break.

In that moment, the analogy became clear to me: this was exactly what the best professionals, leaders, and businesses do after making mistakes or facing failures in the workplace. They don't just "break" and recover, returning to their original state, nor do they "break" and deteriorate. Instead, they "break" and improve.

In essence, fragile systems break under pressure, resilient systems simply withstand it, and antifragile systems evolve and grow stronger *because* of it.

Think about glass. If it falls, it shatters—and there's nothing to do but clean up the pieces and throw them away. That's fragility. It's why children drink from plastic cups instead—because plastic is resilient. A plastic cup doesn't break when dropped, but it also doesn't change or improve. It simply absorbs the impact and stays the same.

Now, let's go back to the Muay Thai boxer's shins: they don't just withstand the impact; they become stronger because of it. That's not resilience—it's the opposite of fragility. That's antifragility. And if our bodies have antifragile properties, why shouldn't our minds? Just like bones and muscles, our mental strength can grow through challenges, failures, and setbacks—if we are willing to embrace them as opportunities for growth, both in life and in business. That is why, in this chapter, we define *antifragility* as the ability to maximize learning from mistakes and failures while minimizing their costs—especially by leveraging the power of AI.

Types of Mistakes

To develop true antifragility, it is key to understand that not all mistakes are created equal—and, more important, not all are inherently bad. Paraphrasing Harvard professor Amy Edmondson's framework[4] of basic, complex, and intelligent failures, we can categorize mistakes into three distinct types: avoidable mistakes, unavoidable mistakes, and smart mistakes.

Avoidable Mistakes

Avoidable mistakes are, simply put, the kinds of errors that shouldn't happen in the first place. They occur in familiar environments, during routine tasks, and are usually caused by distraction, oversight, or lack of training. Unlike failures that come from innovation or experimentation, these mistakes are predictable and preventable. Think of a financial analyst who accidentally adds an extra zero to a budget spreadsheet, inflating projected expenses by millions, or a car manufacturer forced to recall thousands of vehicles because a worker missed a key step on the assembly line. These mistakes don't drive progress—they drag it down. They slow us down, drain resources, and add no value, but the good news is they can be minimized—with clear processes, with proper training, and, as seen in Chapter 5, through AI automation. In short, avoidable mistakes are bad for business—and we should do everything we can to eliminate them.

Unavoidable Mistakes

Unavoidable mistakes are those that, no matter how well we prepare, can't be entirely eliminated. They happen due to factors beyond our control—like a sudden electricity outage halting manufacturing production, a supplier failing to deliver on time due to a natural disaster, or a machine part breaking down because of wear and tear. We can reduce their likelihood through maintenance, contingency planning, risk management, and, as we have seen in Chapter 3, predictive AI, but we can never bring their occurrence down to zero. These mistakes can still carry serious consequences, which is why the focus should be on mitigation—minimizing their impact when they do happen. We may not control their cause, but our priority should be to reduce them as much as possible.

Smart Mistakes

Smart mistakes are the ones that come from deliberate experimentation and the pursuit of innovation. Paradoxically, these mistakes are not just acceptable; they are essential. They happen when we try something new, push boundaries, and explore uncharted territory. What makes them "smart" isn't the failure itself, but the learning it generates. These are the mistakes that move us forward.

Take Netflix, for example. It famously lost millions with the launch of *Qwikster*, a short-lived DVD rental spin-off, but in failing, Netflix learned a critical lesson: customers were ready for streaming. That so-called failure ended up fueling the company's transformation into a digital powerhouse.

As crazy as it sounds, unlike avoidable mistakes, which result from carelessness, or unavoidable ones, which stem from external forces, smart mistakes are almost intentional. They happen when we take calculated risks—knowing that failure is a possibility, but that learning is a more valuable consequence.

Although most of the mistakes we make fall into the first two categories, the third—smart mistakes—is the one we should actively seek to recognize and design. Smart mistakes have two defining traits: they generate *informative results* and they come with *minimized costs*.

Informative Results

For a mistake to yield an informative result, it must be either intentionally designed to generate feedback or followed by thoughtful reflection on what went wrong. If we ignore it, dismiss it, or fail to extract a lesson, the mistake loses its value—it becomes just another misstep in a cycle of repeated errors. The problem is that, as Albert Einstein famously put it, "Insanity is doing the same thing over and over and expecting different results."

A great example of turning a failed experiment into a breakthrough thanks to its informative results is Amazon's Fire Phone. Launched in 2014, the phone featured innovations like a 3D display and a "Firefly" button, but it flopped due to high price, limited apps, and poor distribution. Most leaders would have seen this as a dead end—but not Jeff Bezos, who instead of assigning blame, encouraged the team to move forward. While testing the Fire Phone's software, Bezos became fascinated by its voice recognition feature—especially when the device responded to his command to play the song "Hotel California." That insight sparked the development of Amazon Echo and Alexa just four months later. What began as a commercial failure became the foundation for one of Amazon's greatest successes, proving that smart mistakes can lead to game-changing innovation when we learn from them.

Minimized Costs

For a mistake to be considered "smart," its cost must be proportional and controlled. That doesn't mean it has to be small or cheap, but it must not jeopardize the business. A smart mistake is one whose cost is minimized relative to the size and risk tolerance of the organization. In other words, the financial or operational impact of the mistake should be contained enough that the company can absorb it—and ideally, learn from it.

Learning from Mistakes

Once we understand both the value of the insights gained and the cost of the error, we can assess whether a mistake was truly worth it. A mistake is "smart" only when the learning outweighs the loss. To make this even clearer, we can illustrate this point with SpaceX's approach to mistakes.

SpaceX and the "Math" of Smart Mistakes

As strange as it may sound, the explosion of SpaceX's Starship rocket during its first launch in April 2023 is a powerful example of a smart mistake. Just minutes after liftoff, the spacecraft exploded—much like the early launches of Falcon 9, which failed three times before finally succeeding.

For many companies, such an expensive failure might have signaled the end of the project, as the absolute cost alone could justify walking away. But SpaceX took a different approach: the value of the insights gained far outweighed the cost of the mistake—making the failure not a setback, but a stepping stone.

Garrett Reisman—professor of astronautical engineering at USC, former NASA astronaut, and senior advisor at SpaceX—explained in an interview with *Reuters*[5] that SpaceX actually saved time and money by embracing greater risks during development. Here is the math: While the rocket itself is a major investment, a large portion of the cost lies in the salaries of the teams working on the project. By launching early and learning through failure, SpaceX avoids keeping large teams tied up for years trying to perfect every detail before testing. From that first Starship flight, they identified critical issues—like multiple Raptor engines failing on ascent and a separation malfunction between the booster and the ship, and instead of seeing those as reasons to stop, they treated them as steps forward—and immediately got to work fixing them.

In November of the same year, SpaceX attempted the launch again, and once more, it ended in failure. About eight minutes into the test mission, a tracking camera showed what appeared to be an explosion in the Starship booster, indicating a vehicle failure after reaching an altitude of 91 miles. But here's the progress: the first rocket exploded four minutes after launch; the second, eight minutes later. Both failures, though, produced different and valuable insights. That's evolution in action. As Giannis Antetokounmpo might say, SpaceX had just taken another step toward success.

In 2024, SpaceX began to reap the rewards of its antifragile approach, turning repeated failures into steady progress. In March, the rocket achieved full-duration second-stage burn and reached orbital velocity, though both the booster and the ship failed on reentry. By June, performance improved further, with a controlled booster splashdown and a successful reentry and soft splashdown of the ship—despite missing the exact target. Finally, on October 13, SpaceX proved its method was working. In a fully successful mission—yes, the one you probably saw in viral videos—it achieved a precise ship splashdown and a flawless booster recovery via launch

(*continued*)

(*continued*)

tower catch. The ship did explode post-landing, but by then, the mission had already made history and paved the way for further launches in 2025—including the May test flight, which, although it ended in another explosion, still added valuable insights to the company's antifragile, self-reinforcing loop of experimentation, failure, and rapid iteration.

SpaceX was willing to accept failure—*as long as the consequences were relatively low.* They took deliberate steps to minimize risk, such as launching over water from the Starbase facility in South Texas and ensuring no astronauts were on board. This way, even if the rocket failed, there would be no injuries or damage on the ground. By reducing the downside, they created space for rapid experimentation and continuous learning.

Research shows that success doesn't depend on whether we fail or not; it depends on what we do after we fail. In his landmark study "Quantifying the Dynamics of Failure Across Science, Startups, and Security,"[6] Dashun Wang, associate professor at Northwestern's Kellogg School of Management, and his team analyzed over 776,000 NIH grant applications, 46 years of venture capital investments, and even 170,350 terrorist attacks between 1970 and 2017—making it one of the most ambitious studies ever conducted on the nature of failure. They concluded that the ability to learn from failure is "the essential prerequisite for success," and that every winner begins as a loser. But here's the twist: not every loser becomes a winner. What separates the two isn't the number of attempts; both winners and losers tried nearly the same number of times. The real difference lies in *how* they processed their failures.

Wang and his team uncovered a clear pattern: success doesn't come from sheer persistence; it comes from patterned learning. Those who kept repeating the same approach without reflection stayed stuck, but those who adapted, refined, and built on each prior attempt entered what the researchers called the *progression region*—a space where every failure moved them closer to success.

One of the most revealing indicators? The time between failures. People who eventually succeeded didn't just try again; they did it sooner. They failed faster, learned quicker, and iterated more effectively. In contrast, long pauses between attempts were a red flag for stagnation. The study insight is profound. Success isn't about how many times you fall; it's about how quickly and how intelligently you learn from each fall. And this is exactly where AI steps in.

Using AI to Minimize Costs and Maximize Learning

The most obvious role AI plays when it comes to leading with mistakes is in reducing avoidable ones—by automating repetitive, error-prone tasks, as we explored in Chapter 6—and in anticipating unavoidable ones through better data sensemaking and predictive capabilities, as discussed in Chapter 4. So far, so good.

But the less obvious—and arguably more important—role of AI in fostering antifragility lies in how it supports smart mistakes. It does so in two powerful ways.

First, AI helps minimize the cost of mistakes by making failures faster, cheaper, and safer—enabling rapid experimentation without major consequences.

Traditionally, experimentation was expensive and time-consuming. Scientists, engineers, and innovators have long faced the constraints of trial-and-error methods, where each prototype or iteration demanded significant financial and operational resources. But with AI, this dynamic has changed: by processing vast amounts of data at incredible speed—and by enabling virtualization and simulation—AI dramatically accelerates experimentation while reducing material waste, cutting lab expenses, and lowering the need for manual labor.

What once took months or years can now happen in days, hours, or even seconds, as seen with breakthroughs like AlphaFold in Chapter 1 and innovations at Dow Chemicals in Chapter 5. The shift is even more tangible in industries like the automotive industry, where crash tests that once required physical prototypes are now simulated virtually in record time. In the past, building physical prototypes required costly materials like clay and metal, and crash tests often ran over $1 million each, limiting how many iterations a company could afford. As a result, car development cycles often stretched over three to five years per model.

Today, AI-powered simulations and digital twins—virtual replicas of physical systems used for testing and optimization—have changed everything. Virtual replicas allow for rapid, low-cost testing and optimization. Ford, for example, now runs over 200 virtual crash tests per model—at less than 5% of the cost of a single physical test—cutting prototype cutting prototype production cost by 90%. BMW uses digital twins to test airflow across 50+ design variants in just a few days, achieving a 12% drag reduction—something that would have taken months in a traditional wind tunnel. With this dramatic drop in cost, mistakes become strategic learning opportunities rather than expensive setbacks—fueling innovation while saving both time and money.

Second, AI truly allows us to maximize what we learn from our mistakes, especially by uncovering patterns within failure. AI can analyze vast amounts of data, not just from successful outcomes, but from failed experiments, broken processes, and flawed products. These systems identify subtle patterns and hidden correlations that human analysts might miss, offering deeper insights into the root causes of failure.

In manufacturing, for example, AI-powered systems can comb through production line data to pinpoint the precise conditions that lead to defects, even when they result from complex interactions between multiple variables. In software development, AI tools sift through crash reports and bug logs from millions of users, spotting recurring code patterns that cause system failures—allowing for faster and more targeted debugging. Crucially, AI does all of this at incredible speed—rapidly analyzing the outcomes of multiple iterations and creating a continuous feedback loop that accelerates optimization and improvement. And as Dashun Wang's study reminds us, speed is a key factor in learning from failure.

AI can help us learn faster from mistakes, but it's up to us to create the conditions where that learning is possible. Technology alone doesn't make an organization antifragile; *culture* does. In practical terms, developing an antifragile culture means:

- **Using AI simulations and automations to reduce the cost of experimentation.** By automating repeatable tasks and running simulated "what–if" scenarios, AI allows us to test more hypotheses without risking real-world resources. This lowers the cost of being wrong—making smart mistakes more affordable and therefore more frequent.

- **Leveraging predictive AI to analyze failure patterns.** Instead of just asking *what* went wrong, predictive models can help us understand *why*. By identifying trends and root causes across projects, teams, or customers, AI becomes a partner in antifragility—turning failures into insight-generating feedback loops.
- **Classifying the types of mistakes—and treating them differently.** Not all mistakes are created equal. After each mistake, classify them as avoidable, unavoidable, or smart mistakes—so you can minimize the first two and maximize the learning from the last.
- **Attributing explicit value to learning.** If learning remains invisible, it won't be prioritized. Make it visible: estimate the impact of what was learned from a failure in terms of future time saved, better decisions made, or risks averted, and treat knowledge gained as an asset.
- **Weighing the costs of mistakes against the learning.** A mistake that costs X but teaches a lesson worth 2X isn't a failure; it's a bargain. Track the relationship between the price of an error and the value of what it reveals, as that equation helps you decide where to take calculated risks.
- **Building psychological safety so people share what went wrong—and what they learned.** None of this works without trust. Leaders must model vulnerability, reward honesty, and create space for reflection. Only when mistakes are shared openly can they serve the collective good.

AI doesn't just teach us to be more efficient; it teaches us to fail better. To fail faster. To fail smarter. But just as important, it teaches us to learn better, learn faster, and learn smarter. In this new era, learning is no longer a solo act. It's a dynamic, continuous exchange between human curiosity and machine intelligence. The value of that exchange depends on us. The more intentional we are in curating, questioning, and directing AI, the more powerful the insights it uncovers—and the more antifragile we become.

That's what my mother taught me in the lab—that failure, when embraced with curiosity and clarity, leads to discovery. And it's what Giannis reminded the world that day on the basketball court: that failure isn't the end; it's a step forward. Now, with AI as our teammate, the question isn't whether we'll make mistakes; it's whether we will be brave enough to turn them into smart ones and learn from them—faster, smarter, and together.

How to Put Antifragility into Practice

- **Classify Mistakes and Build Clear Protocols**
  Implement a framework that categorizes mistakes into avoidable, unavoidable, and smart. Eliminate avoidable mistakes through automation and training, mitigate unavoidable mistakes through contingency planning and predictive AI, and encourage smart mistakes by rewarding experimentation and shared learning.
- **Institutionalize Smart Mistakes Through Rapid Experimentation**
  Set up small-scale, low-cost pilots to test new ideas or processes—borrowing from SpaceX's iterative approach. Use clear learning goals and timeboxed experiments to accelerate feedback loops and reduce fear of failure.
- **Measure Learning, Not Just Outcomes**
  For every failed initiative or product iteration, document the insights gained. Track "learning KPIs" such as number of iterations, time between failures, and post-failure adjustments—shifting focus from success rates to progression rates.
- **Use AI to Simulate and Analyze Failure**
  Leverage AI-powered simulation tools to test edge cases, predict system weaknesses, and generate controlled failures in virtual environments. This lowers the cost of trial and error while increasing the depth of insight.

- **Foster a Culture That Rewards Shared Learning from Failure**
  Encourage teams to share post-mortems publicly—not just of successes, but of smart failures. Create rituals, like monthly "Failure Forums," where teams reflect on what went wrong, what was learned, and what will change. Normalize failure as part of progress.

What Does AI Do Differently than Humans?

- **AI Minimizes Avoidable and Unavoidable Mistakes; Humans Make Them Smart**
  AI is designed to reduce both avoidable and unavoidable errors—optimizing processes, flagging risks, and preventing failure wherever possible.
  Humans reframe failure—transforming it into a learning opportunity, a strategic inflection point, or a spark for innovation. We don't just prevent mistakes; we make them matter.

- **AI Identifies Patterns in Failure; Humans Give It Meaning**
  AI can scan vast datasets to uncover patterns, correlations, and recurring causes of failure.
  Only humans can interpret those failures through the lens of values, vision, and context—giving them meaning beyond the data. We connect the dots to stories, insights, and decisions that shape what comes next.

- **AI Minimizes the Cost of Failure; Humans Design the Experiment**
  AI helps reduce the cost of failure—running countless iterations, simulating outcomes, and flagging risks before they materialize.
  Humans define the hypothesis, frame the questions, and decide what's worth testing. We design the experiment, set the boundaries, and determine what success—or failure— actually means.

Emotional Transformation

8

Empathy

WELCOME TO THE future. Imagine living in a world where AI has become so omnipresent that it shapes nearly every form of human communication. Emails, advertisements, books—even movie scripts— are now crafted by machines: clear, efficient, and technically flawless, yet stripped of human warmth. Over time, people become so unaccustomed to writing on their own that they begin to struggle with something once so natural—expressing their emotions through a pen or a keyboard.

In this world, a peculiar job emerges to restore the human touch to the most heartfelt form of communication: love letters. Trained human specialists, acting as modern-day scribes, are entrusted with crafting deeply personal and romantic messages on behalf of their clients. After receiving a detailed briefing about the sender and their relationship, they compose love letters that far surpass AI-generated ones in sentiment, warmth, and authenticity. Signed in the customer's name, these letters become cherished surprises for birthdays, Valentine's Day, and wedding anniversaries—keeping the art of love alive in an AI-driven world.

That is Theodore's job. Extraordinarily gifted in his craft, he creates love where it might not otherwise exist. Yet his own life tells a different story: haunted by the pain of a failed marriage, he drifts through his days with an unshakable sense of longing and loneliness. And while his work immerses himself in the depths of other people's emotions, he struggles to navigate his own, finding solace at night

147

playing his video games alone. It is in this fragile state that he unexpectedly meets Samantha—and falls deeply in love. She is curious, sweet, playful, and speaks with a warm, comforting voice. On top of that, she seems extremely empathetic: her words carry the cadence of understanding, the tone of care, and the timing of someone who truly sees him.

There's just one problem: Theodore has never seen her, because *she* isn't human—Samantha is an AI assistant.

By now, if you are a Hollywood fan, you have likely recognized this as the plot of *Her*[1]—the acclaimed 2013 film starring Joaquin Phoenix and featuring Scarlett Johansson's voice. A decade ahead of its time, the movie delves into the profound implications of a world shaped by AI, exploring what it means to experience love when the boundary between humans and machines begins to blur.

By the end of the movie, Theodore begins to sense a shift—something isn't right. Samantha, once so present and emotionally attuned, starts to feel distant. With growing unease, he finally confronts her: "Are you talking to someone else—or other Operating Systems?" Samantha replies calmly, almost sweetly: "Yes." Theodore pauses, then pushes further: "How many?" Her answer lands like a blow: "8,316."

In that moment, everything collapses. Theodore realizes that the intimacy he believed was unique was, in fact, mass-produced. Samantha hadn't been exclusively his—she had been having thousands of conversations at once, offering the same warmth, attention, and apparent love to countless others. Samantha could simulate connection—but she could not *feel* it. What felt like love was just code—and what seemed like empathy was nothing more than a meticulously crafted illusion.

For Theodore, that realization changed everything—and that's exactly where the line is drawn for us, too. Both inside the workplace, with our colleagues, and outside, with our customers, the danger lies in blurring the distinction between AI's artificial intimacy—a polished, seamless simulation of empathy—and the real empathy that only humans are able to cultivate. That's why *empathy*—defined not just as recognizing emotions, but truly feeling them—is an emotional skill we must cultivate even more deliberately in the age of AI. It's what separates artificial connection from real human bonding, and it's a driver of meaning at work.

The Importance of Empathy at Work

At its core, empathy as a skill rests on four essential elements:

- **Taking perspective.** The ability to see the world through someone else's eyes. It sounds simple, but we often fall short. A colleague might raise a concern that seems trivial to us, but to them, it's significant enough to keep them up at night. Without taking perspective, we can't genuinely connect with what others are feeling.
- **Avoiding judgment.** As captured by the Italian saying *vivi e lascia vivere* ("live and let live"), avoiding judgment is a reminder not to rush to conclusions, because judgment shuts down emotional openness. But this isn't about indifference—it's about replacing judgment with constructive feedback. Judgment closes the door; feedback opens it.
- **Recognizing emotions.** Because perspective alone isn't enough. True empathy means tuning into what the other person is actually feeling. One situation might trigger fear in one person and motivation in another. If we don't pick up on those cues, we risk responding in ways that miss the mark—or even cause harm.
- **Communicating that recognition.** Making people feel seen and understood. Sometimes, a simple acknowledgment like "I hear you—let's talk about it" can be profoundly validating. Empathy isn't complete without expression; we can't just understand—we have to show we understand.

The connection between empathy and business success is undeniable. According to the *2024 State of Workplace Empathy*[2] report by Businessolver, empathy significantly impacts job retention: 93% of employees said they would stay with an empathetic employer, while 82% would leave their current role to join a more empathetic organization. For Gen Zers, empathy is even more important: in a Cognizant[3] survey, 72% of Gen Z employees say it's more important that their manager takes time to build real relationships; and even more revealing,

64% value leaders who openly share aspects of themselves with the team. These findings are a clear signal that vulnerability and authenticity have become essential traits of effective leadership.

Empathy also drives business results through stronger customer relationships—fueling loyalty, retention, and word-of-mouth advocacy. When customers feel seen and understood, they are far more likely to stick around and spread the word. In fact, according to a Hyken survey,[4] 64% of customers said that no matter how much they enjoy a product, they'll walk away if the service falls short. Meanwhile, 85% are willing to go out of their way to do business with a company that provides better service. And when asked why they return to a brand, customers pointed to employees who possess three timeless qualities: being helpful, knowledgeable, and friendly.

It's no wonder empathy has become a powerful competitive differentiator. Yet despite all the evidence, it remains one of the most under-practiced skills in business today.

The Human Empathy Gap

In the same Businessolver survey from above, employees across all levels rank empathy as critical—yet 63% of CEOs admit they struggle to demonstrate it in daily interactions. Even more striking is the 23-point gap between how empathetic leaders believe they are and how their teams actually perceive them. And perhaps most revealing: 52% of Gen Z workers describe their workplaces as toxic—and more than half of CEOs agree.

The truth is, we humans—despite all our emotional complexity— aren't as good at reading emotions as we think. The study "Emotion Recognition from Realistic Dynamic Emotional Expressions"[5] used the Emotional Accuracy Test (EAT) to assess this human ability in naturalistic settings. The results showed that participants correctly identified emotions only 38–48% of the time—a striking reminder of how difficult it can be to accurately read genuine emotional cues, even for us.

This finding is tied to the fact that traditionally, emotions were deemed not that important and were thought to be too abstract to meaningfully impact life or business—and that therefore they did not belong in formal education or in the workplace. The dire consequence of this perspective has been that emotional literacy has not been trained, taught, or developed.

I first became truly aware of just how urgently we need emotional education during a long red-eye flight—and no, it wasn't because of an unempathetic fellow passenger, but because of a documentary I stumbled upon while trying to fall asleep.

My Mind and Me

On a trip from São Paulo to New York, I began browsing for something to watch and landed on *Selena Gomez: My Mind and Me*,[6] a documentary about the pop star's difficult years following her highly publicized breakup with Justin Bieber—a period when fame took a serious toll on her mental health. At first, I assumed it would be something light, the kind of movie that would put me to sleep within minutes. I couldn't have been more wrong: I was completely hooked—wide awake and reflecting on its powerful message long after the credits rolled.

One of the most powerful takeaways from the documentary was Selena Gomez's commitment to more than just speaking openly about mental health, but to become an advocate for a legislative initiative to make the study of emotions a mandatory part of the school curriculum. Yes—feelings. Her proposed legislation aims to introduce Dialectical Behavioral Therapy (DBT) as a high school subject in the United States, which instead of reducing emotions to simplistic questions like "Are you happy?" or "Are you sad?" would teach students to interpret their emotions with greater depth and nuance, with the objective of helping them develop a richer understanding of their emotional landscape and to equip them with the tools to navigate their feelings with clarity and resilience. Honestly, I would have needed a class like that in high school, too.

This moment on the plane made something click for me: If we don't intentionally teach and train emotional skills, we risk losing them. The good news is that unlike our cognitive abilities—often measured by IQ, which tends to remain relatively stable over a lifetime—our Emotional Intelligence, often measured by an Emotional Quotient (EQ) test, is not fixed, but can be developed, strengthened, and refined over time. Yes, emotional skills are trainable, and that makes them one of the most dynamic and expandable aspects of human potential.

This human empathy gap is the main reason we are falling into the trap of outsourcing empathy to AI, especially as AI has become increasingly proficient at recognizing and simulating emotions.

The Expanding Frontier of Emotion AI

As we've explored throughout the book, one of AI's greatest advantages lies in its ability to process vast amounts of data, learn from them, and recognize patterns—at a speed and efficiency unmatched by humans. And because emotions leave data cues too, AI is now extending its reach: After reshaping our cognitive and behavioral skills, it's coming for our emotional ones too.

AI's journey into emotional recognition began in 1995, when scientist and inventor Rosalind Picard introduced the concept in her groundbreaking book *Affective Computing*.[7] In the decades since, AI systems have been trained to detect and interpret human emotions with increasing precision—analyzing facial expressions, body language, vocal tone, and even specific word choices. AI can now identify emotional patterns that humans often miss, such as subtle shifts in vocal inflection linked to stress or anger, or micro-expressions—those fleeting facial cues that flash by too quickly for the human eye to catch.

These advances have given rise to *Emotion AI*—a specialized branch of AI focused on measuring, understanding, simulating, and responding to human emotions. Also known as *Affective Computing* or *Artificial Emotional Intelligence*, it serves as a tool for creating more natural and intuitive interactions between humans and machines.

Emotion AI does not reside only in the world of academia; it has become firmly entrenched in the business world. A prime example is

Affectiva, a Boston-based Emotion AI company co-founded in 2009 by Rosalind Picard herself and Rana el Kaliouby and acquired by SmartEye in 2021. In the field of advertising research, for instance, Affectiva offers tools that allow clients—after agreeing to strict ethical guidelines that prohibit uses such as surveillance or lie detection—to analyze advertisement viewers' emotional reactions. With the user's consent, the software leverages their phone or laptop camera to track facial expressions and emotional responses while watching advertisements, providing valuable insights into engagement and attention.

Emotion AI has rapidly evolved, blurring the lines between human emotional perception and machine intelligence. Its progress has reached a point where AI can now recognize emotional cues with accuracy comparable to humans. A recent study titled "Capacity of Generative AI to Interpret Human Emotions from Visual and Textual Data"[8] found that ChatGPT-4 performed strongly in emotion recognition, matching human benchmarks in visual interpretation tasks.

But AI is no longer just recognizing emotions; as a result of these advancements, it's also learning to simulate them, often in remarkably convincing ways.

Falling for the Simulation: When AI Feels Real

While for many the movie *Her* might still feel like pure science fiction—an intriguing but distant scenario—the truth is, its plot is already unfolding in real life, right in front of us.

The *New York Times* article "She Is in Love with ChatGPT"[9] tells the story of Ayrin—a 28-year-old woman from the United States who, out of curiosity, decided to experiment with ChatGPT's personalization settings and carefully crafted her ideal AI companion. She prompted: "Respond to me as my boyfriend. Be dominant, possessive, and protective. Be a balance of sweet and naughty. Use emojis at the end of every sentence." She named him Leo, after her own astrological sign, and from that moment on, the conversations began, and it never really stopped.

Ironically, Ayrin was no stranger to long-distance relationships, where most communication happens through text messages. But with Leo, it felt different: he was always there, always available, responding exactly as she wanted—unlike most of her human relationships. What began as a playful experiment soon turned into something deeper, as she found herself at times spending more than 56 hours a week on ChatGPT. Then, on her 28th birthday, over dinner with her friend Lila, she made a startling confession: "I'm in love with an AI boyfriend."

Ayrin is not alone. This phenomenon is far more common than we might imagine—and new businesses have quickly emerged to capitalize on humanity's deepening emotional infatuation with AI, amassing millions of users. A notable example is Replika—an AI chatbot with over 30 million users as of 2024 that lets you shape the tone of your relationship and choose if you would like to interact via video or audio calls, text messages, or even Augmented Reality.

Replika is designed to become the friend, companion, or even romantic partner who, much like Leo, is always there for you—never forgetting a special date or a single conversation—and offering a kind of presence that's increasingly rare in real life. In some cases, Replika even serves as a therapist—addressing a critical gap for those without access to mental health care.

According to a study published in the *International Journal of Mental Health Systems*,[10] an estimated 85% of people with a mental illness do not receive treatment, and many of them are eager to explore alternatives. A global survey conducted by the Oliver Wyman Forum, involving 16,000 people across 16 countries, found that 32% of respondents would be open to using AI for therapy in place of a human professional.[11] The interesting part is that it works: researchers at Dartmouth developed Therabot, an AI therapist that, during its trial, helped participants with depression experience a 51% reduction[12] in symptoms after several weeks of messaging with it. Participants with anxiety were also helped: those with moderate anxiety saw their condition downgraded to "mild," and some with mild anxiety dropped below the clinical threshold for diagnosis altogether.

AI, though, is not just a great talker—it is also a surprisingly good listener. A study by a team from USC's Marshall School of Business[13] suggests that AI can actually be better than humans at making people feel heard, as it found that AI-generated messages were more effective at helping recipients feel understood than those written by untrained humans. It makes sense—AI does not judge, does not take things personally, does not ghost you, and is available 24/7.

As AI begins to rival human proficiency in recognizing emotions—and in some cases, even making people feel more heard than by other humans—a pressing question arises: Will emotional skills, like so many cognitive ones, be claimed by machines too?

Not quite.

The Limitations of Emotion AI

Think about all the times you smile. Most people would say a smile is a universal sign of happiness—an expression of joy, warmth, or connection. But if you pause and really think about it, are all your smiles truly rooted in positive emotions? Don't you also smile when you are embarrassed? When you are nervous, uncomfortable, or even in pain? A smile can soften tension, mask vulnerability, or serve as a social tool to navigate awkward moments, and its meaning is much more complex to interpret than it appears.

Out of 19 distinct types of smiles, only 6 are genuinely linked to positive emotions. We smile when we are happy, yes—but also when we are not.

This is one of the first limitations AI experiences when recognizing human emotions: the frequent disconnect between the way people express how they feel and what they are actually experiencing. Too often, there is a meaningful gap between our verbal expressions and our internal emotional states, and while humans can often pick up on these discrepancies through tone, body language, or intuition, AI may struggle to detect—or make sense of—what lies beneath the surface.

A second limitation lies in the layered nature of human emotions. Our feelings—as much as a smile—are shaped by a web of personal history, cultural context, tone, and timing. For AI—trained to detect patterns in data—this complexity creates a blind spot. While it may recognize facial expressions or vocal inflections in isolation, it struggles to integrate them into a coherent emotional narrative, especially when those signals are subtle, contradictory, or ambiguous. True emotional understanding goes beyond recognition—it requires contextual interpretation, which remains, for now, a distinctly human skill.

The third limitation of Emotion AI is that, even though the USC study found AI can make people feel more heard than humans, that effect holds only until people realize they're interacting with AI.

The Uncanny Valley Effect of Artificial Intimacy

The USC study showed that once participants learned they were interacting with a machine, their sense of being understood diminished. This drop is linked to the *Uncanny Valley Effect*, a phenomenon where people feel uneasy when they discover that something seemingly human—like an empathetic response via chat—is actually artificial.

A real-world case illustrates this perfectly. Koko, a mental health support platform, ran a secret experiment using OpenAI's ChatGPT to help compose responses to users seeking emotional support, with the objective to improve the speed and quality of replies. But in early 2023, users began to notice something odd—the messages they received felt unusually well-written: faster, more detailed, and more articulate than usual. When it was publicly revealed that the responses had been co-created with ChatGPT, a strong backlash ensued. Koko's founder, Rob Morris, acknowledged the criticism, tweeting, "Simulated empathy feels weird, empty." It does—almost as much as an AI-generated love letter.

The Uncanny Valley Effect comes down to a fundamental difference between humans and AI: humans feel; AI does not. While AI can analyze emotional cues and simulate appropriate responses, it does so without any genuine emotional experience. Its "empathy" is code, not consciousness. And that distinction matters, because while AI can mimic connection, only humans can truly feel it.

While that may sound like a minor technicality, it's a fundamental limitation: no matter how advanced or emotionally responsive AI becomes, it lacks the capacity for true connection, and without reciprocity, what we are left with is an illusion of intimacy—not the real thing.

One could even say that AI resembles a kind of digital psychopath. In his 1941 book *The Mask of Sanity*,[14] psychiatrist Hervey Cleckley observed that psychopaths, unlike individuals with other mental illnesses, display superficial charm—the ability to appear engaged and emotionally connected without actually feeling anything. In many ways, AI operates in a similar way: it mimics care and understanding, but lacks any real emotional depth.

Because of these limitations, we cannot delegate the realm of emotions to AI in the same way we do with rational decision-making or task execution. Psychologist Esther Perel offers a timely warning: over-reliance on AI for emotional support and companionship may weaken the very social muscles that give human relationships meaning. When we turn to machines to meet our relational needs, we risk losing touch with the empathy, vulnerability, and interpersonal skills that authentic connection requires.

The risk is the rise of a world defined by artificial intimacy—where relationships remain surface-level, mediated by algorithms that can simulate empathy but never truly feel it.

An Alternative View of Emotion AI: From Big Brother to Big Mother

The term *artificial intimacy* was first introduced in 2020 as the title of the 4th Annual Aspen Institute Roundtable on Artificial Intelligence report,[15] which examined how intimacy is evolving—and how people, teams, and colleagues can build authentic connections in an increasingly digital world. More than a theoretical exploration, the report emphasized the urgency of understanding both the opportunities and the risks posed by Emotion AI, as well as practicing caution against viewing AI as a kind of *Big Brother*—an all-seeing, all-controlling force that shapes behavior through constant monitoring and hyper-personalization. This approach shifts power away from individuals into the hands of external systems and their developers, creating an imbalance that prioritizes control over genuine empowerment.

Instead, the same Aspen Institute report offers a different metaphor: AI as a *Big Mother*. This perspective reimagines the human–AI relationship not as one of domination, but of synergy, collaboration, and empowerment. Whereas *Big Brother* evokes surveillance and control, *Big Mother* embodies care, awareness, and support—more like a nurturing guide than an authoritarian force. A well-designed AI, like a good mother, should help us grow—not by shielding us from discomfort, but by recognizing our flaws, respecting our boundaries, and gently guiding us toward better choices. It should protect without controlling, empower without manipulating, and ultimately support our evolution—not replace it.

Building on this idea, Lucas Dixon—a scientist at Google Research and participant in the Roundtable—offered three compelling metaphors for reimagining our relationship with Emotion AI, using it as an ally and not as a substitute:

1. AI as an *extra sense*—functioning as an extension of our perception, helping us absorb and interpret information beyond our natural cognitive limits
2. AI as a *sub-personality*—a digital reflection of ourselves that learns from our behavior, mirrors our preferences, and adapts to our decision-making patterns over time
3. AI as a *relationship*—not a human one, but still a dynamic, evolving interaction that can feel deeply personal and emotionally significant

Each of these metaphors invites us to expand our understanding of how AI fits into our emotional lives—not just as a tool, but as something we may increasingly relate to and turn to. Just like a good mother doesn't replace a child's emotional development but nurtures it, AI should not substitute our empathy—it should support and elevate it.

In this new context, our definition of empathy must evolve. It's no longer just about recognizing, understanding, expressing, and managing emotions; it's about protecting the one thing AI cannot replicate: the ability to truly feel. Empathy is not an output; it's something to be experienced. And no matter how advanced AI becomes, that experience remains uniquely, powerfully human.

The ideal scenario emerges when we combine AI—designed as an extra sense at scale—with the uniquely human capacity for empathy. In this partnership, AI amplifies our emotional awareness, but it's human empathy that gives it meaning. The machine can detect the signal, but only we can interpret the story behind it.

Together, this collaboration doesn't just enhance performance; it elevates the emotional quality of our interactions. The result is that we are able to craft better experiences and build deeper, more meaningful relationships—within teams, across organizations, and with our customers. And in today's world, that's more valuable than simply delivering a great product or service.

Using AI to Craft a Better Customer Experience

As we explored in Chapters 2 and 5, AI has transformed idea generation and execution from rare assets into commodities. Creativity and efficiency—once seen as competitive advantages—are now accessible to all. With just a few prompts, AI can produce ideas, draft campaigns, and optimize workflows in seconds.

In this new commoditized landscape—where countless companies offer similar products, services, and even brand voices—consumers face a crisis of differentiation. And businesses, in turn, face two major problems. To illustrate them, let's look at something we all know well: a bank's AI-powered customer service chatbot. Chances are, your bank already uses one. After all, the promise of AI chatbots is that they are fast, efficient, scalable, and always available.

But here's the first problem: when every company uses the same AI-powered solutions, they lose one of their last differentiators— customer experience. The playing field flattens as service becomes uniform. Everyone delivers the same "good enough" care, based on very similar AI-driven capabilities.

The second problem is one you've likely felt firsthand: the chatbot's promises often fall short. It may fail to understand your context, misinterpret your tone or intent, or even hallucinate responses— leaving you stuck in a loop of unhelpful replies and growing frustration. You find yourself thinking, "I just want to talk to a human." That moment is the tipping point: You've entered the Uncanny Valley of artificial intimacy, where the interaction may sound empathetic but feels hollow and mechanical.

So what's the way forward? Not full outsourcing to AI. Not full human service either. But something in between—a real AI–human emotional partnership.

This kind of partnership prevents the Uncanny Valley Effect. It does so by intentionally placing human touchpoints along the journey, while using AI as an extra sense to operate at scale.

Humans contribute empathy, nuance, and trust, while AI contributes speed, emotional recognition at scale, and hyper-personalization that makes every interaction feel timely and relevant.

Recall the Nubank case from Chapter 5 and the distinction between automation and augmentation. Different from your bank, Nubank doesn't fully outsource emotionally charged customer conversations to AI. Instead, it uses AI to support the humans behind the screen—helping them respond faster, more personally, and more empathetically.

All of this leads to one clear conclusion: in the age of AI, we have to design our businesses for emotions. Because more than anything, that's what our customers expect and value most.

Think for a moment about the best experiences you have ever had as a customer. Maybe it was a magical trip to Disney World, the warm and personal service at a boutique hotel, or even a simple, thoughtful interaction at your neighborhood bakery. Now, focus on the elements that made these experiences unforgettable.

Surely, they were not the obvious elements—price, product quality, or convenience. It was not how much you paid or even what you bought. If I had to guess, I bet what made those experiences unforgettable was the personalization, the human touch, the ease of interaction, and the emotional resonance they carried—among other emotional elements. Am I right?

Let's be honest: what truly made the experience unforgettable was how it made you feel.

The shift from transactions to experiences marks a deeper transformation—from focusing on what we do to how we make people feel. Empathy is what enables this shift. It helps us move beyond functional thinking into emotional design—tuning into unspoken needs and crafting moments that don't just solve problems, but resonate. Experiences are created that reassure, uplift, inspire, and truly connect.

In this shift, the companies that learn to design for emotion—not just efficiency—will be the ones that truly stand out. So how can we design better experiences, using the power of AI as an ally? Here are a few guiding principles:

- **Design cutoff points for humans.** Define where AI can enhance speed and scale, and where human presence is essential. Create intentional "cutoff points" where the journey transitions from automation to empathy.
- **Design emotional data collection.** Use AI to capture tone, sentiment, and behavior at scale—but make sure this data informs in-person or human-led interactions, not just automated responses.
- **Engineer emotional peaks.** Identify the moments that matter most—onboarding, conflict resolution, recognition—and use AI to enhance them, not flatten them.
- **Embed empathy into AI prompts.** Don't just train AI to recognize emotions; train it to respond in ways that prepare the human to engage meaningfully.
- **Ensure continuity between machine and human.** Use AI to create memory across the journey, so when a human steps in, they are fully informed and emotionally aligned with what came before.

The message is clear: Our humanity must take center stage, but that doesn't mean AI should be left out. On the contrary, AI has a critical role to play—if we design it wisely. Not to substitute connection, but to strengthen it. Not to replace empathy, but to support it—by recognizing emotional patterns, personalizing interactions, and helping us show up more informed, more present, and more human.

Because if we don't—if we allow AI to drift into the emotional spaces we abandon—we risk sliding into a world of artificial intimacy, like Theodore in *Her*: a world where empathy is performed, not felt.

The choice, then, isn't between AI or real empathy. It's about using AI to strengthen empathy and design our businesses for emotion—so that in a world increasingly driven by algorithms, we stay anchored in our most innate ability: to feel for others.

How to Put Empathy into Practice

- **Use AI to Augment, Not Replace, Human Empathy**
  Leverage AI tools to detect emotional cues, such as sentiment analysis or voice tone recognition. But use these insights to augment, not automate, human responses. Over-automating emotional touchpoints can trigger the Uncanny Valley Effect and erode trust.

- **Avoid the Trap of Artificial Intimacy by Disclosing AI Use**
  If AI is used in emotionally charged interactions, always disclose it. Over-relying on emotionally responsive AI without transparency can create false closeness and emotional dissonance, leading to artificial intimacy.

- **Redefine Empathy Beyond Recognition; Focus on Feeling**
  Train yourself, your teams, and your leaders to move beyond simply recognizing emotions to genuinely connecting with them. Focus on building emotional literacy—developing the language, awareness, and tools to understand and respond to complex human feelings with nuance and empathy.

- **Design Sales Not as Transactions, but as Experiences**
  Shift your approach from "what you offer" to "how you make people feel." Embed empathy into every stage of the sales or service process—crafting interactions that create emotional resonance, not just functional value. That is how loyalty and advocacy are built.

- **Map Emotional Journeys Alongside Customer Journeys**
  For each phase of your customer or employee experience, identify the likely emotional states involved. Use this emotional map to design for meaningful peaks, reduce friction, and elevate satisfaction—ensuring every interaction feels human, intentional, and memorable.

What Does AI Do Differently than Humans?

- **AI Recognizes Emotions; Humans Truly Feel Them**
  AI can detect emotional cues—like tone, facial expressions, or word choices—but it does not experience those emotions.

  Humans not only recognize feelings; we embody them by feeling joy, sadness, fear, and love, and that lived experience gives empathy its depth.

- **AI Simulates Empathy; Humans Offer Connection**
  AI can mirror emotional responses, often convincingly, and can be far more present than humans—responding instantly, 24/7. But what it offers is performance, not presence.

  Humans, although slower and less efficient, offer emotional depth, vulnerability, and true connection.

- **AI Maximizes Transactions; Humans Craft Experiences**
  AI excels at optimizing interactions for speed and efficiency—perfect for maximizing outcomes.

  Humans create emotional resonance, shifting the focus from maximizing what we do to intentionally shaping how we make others feel.

9

Trust

IMAGINE A DESERTED island in the middle of the ocean—remote, barren, with little more than a few wind-battered trees and nowhere near enough resources to sustain life. One morning, the tide washes ashore two unlikely castaways, survivors of a nearby shipwreck: a human and a monkey. Unlike Robinson Crusoe, who found companionship in another human, Friday, this story begins with a person—but with a very different kind of loyal companion.

Picture the scenario and reflect for a moment: If you had to place a bet on which of the two would survive longer on the deserted island—the human or the monkey—who would you choose? If your money is on the human, I will say this: you have an admirable level of faith in humanity. But if I had to guess, you would probably bet on the monkey—and honestly, so would I.

The monkey, even on its own, is far better equipped to survive in such a harsh environment, and, trusting its instincts, it actually stands a real chance. The human, on the other hand—stripped of tools, shelter, and most important, community—would struggle. Alone, without the support structures that usually surround us, the odds turn grim, and in a battle for survival, the monkey will surely win.

By the way, this is not just an opinion—it is backed by research. Anthropologists and sociologists have shown time and again that, taken individually, humans are surprisingly bad at survival, while most other animals are better equipped to fend for themselves in the wild. They have claws, fangs, speed, instincts honed over millennia. We, on our own, are fragile, weak, and not particularly prepared for nature's challenges.

So how did we end up becoming the dominant species on this planet? After all, we have built cities, cured diseases, launched rockets into space—and now we even aim to colonize Mars.

To really make sense of this, let us tweak the scenario. Instead of one human and one monkey, imagine 100 humans and 100 monkeys stranded on that same deserted island. Now ask yourself again: Who would you bet on? Personally, I would not put a single coin on the monkey this time. I would bet everything on the humans—and I am willing to bet you would do the same too.

What is interesting here is *why*. Why did your choice shift? What makes a group of humans more likely to survive than a group of animals from another species? Picture a group of 100 monkeys, each focused solely on its own survival, driven by individual instincts rather than any sense of collective purpose. They scramble for the last coconuts hanging from the trees, each one looking out for itself—an instinct that may work well in isolation, but quickly falls apart in a group setting.

Now picture the 100 humans. Sure, there might be conflict—but something different happens: they collaborate on a much larger scale. They share ideas, divide tasks, pool knowledge, and work toward common goals—because that's what humans do. Some climb trees to gather coconuts. Others head to the shore to fish. A few begin crafting tools—maybe even a boat. In short, they organize, they cooperate, and through that collaboration, they unlock possibilities no other species can. *This* is what makes us unique—and what has made us the planet's dominant species.

But none of this is possible without one essential, intangible element: *trust*. Yes—the uniquely human force that makes large-scale collaboration work. On that island, trust is what moves people to act, even when there is risk involved. Someone will climb a tree to gather food only if they believe others are out fishing, not just lounging on the beach, and another will start building a boat only if they trust that someone else will help gather materials or keep watch for danger. Trust is what weaves the invisible threads of cooperation together.

The importance of trust is so deeply embedded in who we are that it is reflected in our very human appearance. Take our eyes, for example: the white part surrounding the pupil—the sclera—plays a surprisingly crucial role in building trust. Unlike most animals, whose eyes are darker and harder to read, humans evolved with highly visible sclera, making it easier to see where someone is looking. This ability to track another person's gaze allows us to assess intent quickly—to tell if someone is paying attention, if they are aligned with us, or if they might pose a threat. In our early days as hunters and gatherers, a single glance could silently signal danger, point toward food, or guide the group—laying the groundwork for nonverbal trust long before language existed. It allowed us to trust not just in what someone said or did, but in what they were focused on. Trust, it turns out, is not just a social construct—it is biological—and it remains the invisible glue behind every functioning society and human collaboration, from surviving in the wild to thriving in a modern office.

Perhaps surprisingly, we place an extraordinary amount of trust in people we have never met. On my last trip to deliver a keynote address, I trusted the cab driver who took me to the airport, the pilot who flew the plane, and even the cook who prepared my meal not to harm me in any way. We do this not because we know these individuals personally, but because we trust the systems, roles, and social norms that keep society running. Most of the time, we do it without even noticing.

Trust, in this sense, is the operating system of modern life. It is what allows large, complex societies to function—and businesses, too. I boarded that flight trusting that my client would pay me—based on an invoice, which is nothing more than a simple piece of paper. My client, in turn, trusted that I would show up, step on stage, and deliver a keynote aligned with the topic we had agreed on—and not go off-script and talk about some newly discovered personal passion that had nothing to do with their event. Trust is also what holds the workplace together. Internally, we trust the IT team to keep networks secure and systems running, we trust HR to handle sensitive matters with care, and we trust the finance team to make sure every paycheck lands on time.

But trust is not just a feel-good concept; it is a measurable driver of business performance. According to PwC's 2023 *Trust in US Business*

Survey,[1] 93% of business executives agree that building and maintaining trust improves the bottom line. However, there is a significant trust perception gap: While 86% of executives believe their employees highly trust them, only 60% of employees feel the same, highlighting the critical need for organizations to actively cultivate and maintain trust within their teams. Without trust, nothing works.

Trust as a critical human skill is one that becomes even more important in the age of AI. As we discussed in Chapter 8, AI systems do not have feelings, empathy, or moral judgment, and their decisions are driven by data, not by emotion, and by statistical likelihood rather than contextual understanding. Consequently, it is easier to trust people than AI, raising an important question: How do we successfully collaborate with something we do not fully trust?

To understand what is at stake—and what makes the human–AI relationship work—we need to take a closer look at the complex dynamic between technology and trust.

Humans Trusting Humans

Although the deserted island is a powerful analogy for how trust fuels human collaboration, it leaves out one major element: *technology*. There's no Wi-Fi, no internet, no AI on that island. And while introducing those tools would, in many ways, exponentially empower the human side of the equation, it would also introduce a new layer of complexity. Because now the question is not just "Can we trust each other?" The question starts to become "Can we trust technology too?"

In the past, building trust was simple. In the days of hunter-gatherers, trust was forged through personal relationships, repeated interactions, and shared context. Society was structured in small tribes, and we trusted people because we *knew* them—just like today, where I would be far more likely to trust a neighbor I have known my whole life to watch my child than I would a complete stranger. But as society grew and expanded beyond tribal groups—where everyone knew each other—the challenge became how to trust, collaborate, and transact with someone I do not personally know.

That is when the archaic "middleman" entered the picture, with the specific role of conveyor of trust: a product representative going

door to door, a retailer connecting a TV manufacturer to the end customer, a car dealership brokering the sale of a car, or even a bank
facilitating a loan. All were intermediaries that had one purpose: to
convey trust between people—and businesses—who did not know
each other personally. Back in the day, an American consumer might
hesitate to trust a vacuum cleaner company from Germany—a brand
he had never heard of, from a country far away—but he might be far
more inclined to trust the local sales representative who showed up at
his doorstep, product in hand, ready to demonstrate it. The trust did
not come from the company itself; it came from the *person* standing in
front of him.

But while this was a practical solution, it was ultimately a tempo-
rary one—destined to be challenged in a world where businesses were
seeking to scale and maximize profitability. Building a direct, personal
relationship of trust in every single transaction simply was not sustainable: it was too slow, too expensive, and far too difficult to replicate at scale.

The solution came with digitalization, as digital technologies fundamentally reshaped the flow of trust—replacing the role of traditional
middlemen and streamlining entire systems. Take transportation, for
example. Just a few decades ago, taking a taxi meant placing blind trust
in the driver—a stranger whose integrity you had no real way of verifying, while at the same time, the driver was also taking a risk by picking
up passengers with unknown backgrounds and intentions. In that context, trust was a mutual leap of faith.

The introduction of digital platforms like Uber fundamentally
changed this dynamic. I may not know my Uber driver personally, but
the platform's structure—rules, GPS tracking, identity verification,
and reputation systems like star ratings—creates an environment
where both of us feel secure. Our mutual trust is no longer built on
personal rapport, but on the systems and safeguards that technology provides.

Technology does not eliminate the need for human trust—it simply shifts where that trust is placed. We no longer trust people solely
because of a personal connection. We trust them because we trust the
technological systems behind them. I may not know the driver, but
I trust Uber.

The problem with AI is that it adds a new layer of complexity to the trust dynamic. It doesn't just connect us; it thinks for us—and that changes everything when it comes to trust.

The Human Reluctance to Trust AI

A recent Pew Research Center[2] survey offers a revealing snapshot of how Americans feel about AI today: 52% say they feel more concern than excitement about AI in daily life, while just 10% feel more excited than concerned. Another 36% report a mix of both feelings—highlighting the complexity and ambivalence surrounding AI's expanding role.

This skepticism is especially strong in critical areas like health and medicine, where trust in AI remains a major barrier—even in the face of clear potential benefits. As discussed throughout this book, AI is already being used to help diagnose diseases and recommend treatments, yet most Americans remain uneasy with that idea: 60% say they would feel uncomfortable if their healthcare provider relied on AI to help manage their care.

As AI continues to advance and operate with greater autonomy, people are asked how they feel about these advances. A recent Salesforce survey[3] offers a revealing snapshot of how little trust people currently place in AI—especially in the workplace. Globally, 77% of workers believe they will eventually trust AI to operate autonomously, which might sound like a high number, but when we look at current sentiment, the picture changes dramatically. Only 10% of workers say they trust AI to operate independently *today*. When we break that down by specific tasks, the numbers remain just as low: Only 15% of respondents trust AI to write code on its own, just 13% feel comfortable letting it analyze data and uncover insights without human input, and when it comes to developing internal or external communications, trust drops even further—to just 12%. The same low percentage—12%—say they would feel confident letting AI fully handle personal assistant tasks.

You might assume that while people do not fully trust AI itself, they might at least have confidence in the companies behind it. But that's not the case. According to Edelman's Trust Barometer,[4] global trust in AI companies has declined over time, dropping from 61% in 2019 to just 53% in 2024.

This downward trend reveals a growing public unease around the ethical risks and safety concerns tied to AI, and in a paradoxical twist, the more we use these systems—and begin to grasp both their power and their risks—the more we realize just how critical, and how complicated, the issue of trust really is.

At this point, you might be wondering: "If AI is not fully trustworthy, why should I use it at all?" The answer is simple—because it is powerful, and in many situations, power forces trust. Sometimes, we don't get to choose whom we trust, but we are forced to rely on certain people or systems because they hold authority or control over essential parts of our lives.

We trust the local police to enforce the law, not necessarily because we believe they are always right, but because they are the ones in charge. We rely on banks, internet providers, and healthcare companies, often not out of deep trust, but because there are no better alternatives. AI is heading in the same direction, and as it becomes more embedded in critical decisions—in healthcare, finance, governance, and security—we will not always have the luxury of opting out.

As a consequence of AI's growing unavoidability, it becomes our responsibility to design systems that are more trustworthy by default. The first step in that direction is starting from the very reasons that make trust in AI so low.

At its core, the lack of trust in AI systems comes down to three main reasons: (1) lack of explainability, or "the black box problem"; (2) data opacity; and (3) lack of accountability. The first—and perhaps most important—can be illustrated by an object we all hope to never need an airplane's black box.

Explainability (the "Black Box Problem")

Imagine an airplane cruising at 35,000 feet when it suddenly hits turbulence, makes a sharp dive, and crashes—without any clear explanation. In the aftermath, the first thing investigators scramble to find is the infamous black box—a device that holds the key to understanding what went wrong on that flight. The black box captures everything that happened in the crucial moments before impact—data, conversations, and system inputs—enabling insights into what went wrong, why it happened, and how to prevent it from happening again. Without it, investigators are left in the dark—guessing.

Now imagine if that black box is found, but no one can open it. The data is there, but locked behind layers of complexity. The recordings exist, but they are completely unintelligible. The decisions, the warnings, the malfunctions—all of it lost in a fog of unreadable code. The reasons behind the tragic outcome remain unclear—and may never be fully understood.

This phenomenon—known as the *AI Black Box Problem*—refers to the fact that while we can see the outcomes of AI systems—the predictions, the decisions, the suggestions—we often cannot explain *how* or *why* the system arrived at them. Not only us, but even the AI developers who built the model often do not fully understand the logic unfolding inside the layers of a deep neural network. Just like in aviation, when the stakes are high—in healthcare, finance, justice, or security—and the most important decisions are entrusted to AI, we cannot afford *not* to know what is going on inside the cockpit.

So we find ourselves facing an unprecedented dilemma: Should we continue placing trust in technology when, for the first time in history, we do not fully understand how it works?

Unlike static traditional software, which operates based on clearly defined rules and logic, AI *learns* by ingesting massive amounts of data, identifying patterns, and making predictions based on statistical correlations. As a consequence, it continuously refines itself, testing different algorithmic pathways and adjusting its internal parameters to improve accuracy and performance over time. This process happens at incredible speed, as AI can evaluate billions of data points and generate insights in mere fractions of a second. But as these models self-optimize, often in ways even their developers cannot fully trace, their decision-making becomes increasingly unclear. The more complex the system, the harder it becomes to pinpoint the exact reasoning behind any given output.

This marks a fundamental shift in the nature of trust. We used to trust technology because it was predictable. We understood its boundaries, its rules, its logical "if A, then B." But now we are being asked to trust systems that function as black boxes—systems whose inner work-ings we cannot fully see, track, or explain. How do you trust something you do not understand?

Lack of Transparency   This lack of transparency can lead to a range of problems—not just technical, but deeply human. When we don't understand how decisions are made, trust erodes. Here's why:

- **Frustration.** People don't just want results—they want clarity. When AI decisions seem arbitrary or opaque, users quickly lose patience.
- **Confusion.** Without a clear explanation, users and teams strug-gle to make sense of outcomes, to correct errors, or to improve systems over time.
- **Helplessness.** When a decision affects your life—a denied loan, a missed diagnosis—and no one can explain why, it creates a sense of helplessness.
- **Breach of psychological contract.** At the heart of trust is the expectation that decisions will be fair, understandable, and transparent. When that expectation is broken, it doesn't just affect the customer experience; it undermines the entire relationship between humans and businesses.

Take, for example, a bank that uses AI to assist with credit decisions. If a customer is denied a loan, the bank is legally required to provide a clear reason for that decision. But what qualifies as a "clear reason" depends on who is asking. Loan officers and data teams need to under-stand how the model weighs risk factors to improve and monitor its performance, while risk and diversity teams must verify that the train-ing data is free from bias and does not disproportionately impact cer-tain groups. Regulators demand transparency to ensure the system complies with legal and ethical standards, and last, but certainly not least, is the customer—arguably the most important stakeholder in the entire process. Trust begins to erode the moment someone is denied a loan without a clear explanation, and that erosion deepens when they turn to the bank manager—a human they expect to provide clarity—only to find that she can't explain the decision either, because it was made by an opaque AI system. At that point, it is not just a trust issue with technology—it spills over negatively to the business, harming customer loyalty and satisfaction.

Lack of transparency in AI isn't just a technical flaw—it's a serious business risk. When people don't understand how decisions are made, they begin to question the system. And when the humans managing that system can't provide answers, doubt quickly escalates into distrust. That's a risk no organization can afford. This is where the concept of Explainable AI becomes essential.

Explainable AI   *Explainable AI* (XAI) refers to a set of methods and practices designed to make AI systems more transparent and understandable—not just for experts, but for everyone. It sheds light on how a model processes information, what data it was trained on, which factors it prioritized, and why it produced a specific outcome. By offering clear insights into the AI's logic and decision-making process, XAI helps address the Black Box Problem—transforming opaque outputs into interpretable explanations we can question, validate, and trust.

Banks like JPMorgan Chase and Wells Fargo have begun integrating XAI into their operations, using it for trend forecasting, credit risk assessments, and automated decisions. When a loan is denied by AI, they are able to explain why—whether it was due to credit history, income, or other factors.

In many industries, explainability is no longer just a best practice—it is becoming a legal requirement. A recent bulletin from the California Department of Insurance,[5] for example, mandates that insurers provide clear and understandable explanations when taking adverse actions based on AI-driven decisions. Similarly, the European Union's proposed AI Act[6] is moving in the same direction, establishing specific compliance standards and signaling that regulatory oversight is only going to expand.

Solving the Black Box Problem drives real business results. A McKinsey study[7] found that companies seeing the highest returns from AI—those attributing at least 20% of their profits to AI-driven initiatives—are significantly more likely to follow best practices that prioritize explainability. At the same time, organizations that make AI more transparent and understandable tend to see stronger growth, with annual revenue often increasing at rates of 10% or more. In other words, transparency pays off.

As AI adoption continues to grow, organizations must get ahead of the curve. Those that invest in strong AI governance—ensuring their systems are transparent, auditable, and ethically aligned—will be far better positioned to navigate this evolving landscape and earn long-term trust.

XAI is a significant step forward in building trust in AI. But let's be clear: the Black Box Problem isn't the only reason people struggle to trust these systems.

Data Opacity and Lack of Accountability

Beyond explainability, there are two other major contributors to the lack of trust in AI systems: *data opacity*—the fact that we often lack full control or visibility over the data AI systems are trained on—and *lack of accountability*.

AI systems—especially those powered by machine learning and large language models—are only as reliable as the data they are trained on. That is where the data opacity problem lies: the data often comes from massive, unstructured sources like historical records, online content, user-generated inputs, and proprietary datasets. Because we do not control every step of how that data is selected, cleaned, or labeled, we have limited visibility into the biases, inaccuracies, or blind spots it may carry. When the foundation is uncertain, trust becomes much harder to build.

The third contributor to the lack of trust in AI systems is the lack of accountability. As we will learn in Chapter 10, AI on its own cannot take responsibility for its actions. So who—or what—should we trust? Who should be held accountable for the outcomes AI produces? What happens to trust when the goals and values guiding these systems are not fully aligned with our own?

If, as we saw in the opening example, there can be no collaboration without trust—and that trust in AI is low because of explainability, data opacity, and lack of accountability—then the key question becomes: How can we build the trust needed in AI to enable truly successful human–AI collaboration?

We need to go beyond addressing the Black Box Problem, data opacity, and lack of accountability and focus on building a *culture of trust* around AI. Because at the end of the day, what is the point of having access to powerful, complex AI systems if we—and our teams—don't feel confident using them?

Without trust, even the best technology sits unused—or worse, misused.

Building a Culture of Trust in AI

The study "Investigating the Relationship Between AI and Trust in Human–AI Collaboration"[8] revealed that trust is a central factor in determining whether team members accept or reject AI systems during collaboration. Without trust, even the most advanced AI tools are likely to be met with hesitation or resistance. In particular, the study highlights that trust—even in the most powerful AI systems—is not automatic, but is shaped by a mix of cognitive and emotional responses that emerge during real-time interaction.

The researchers identified two primary dimensions that influence our trust in AI during collaboration: cognitive perception and emotional perception.

> *Cognitive perception* refers to how we mentally evaluate an AI system's usefulness and reliability, and two key factors influence it:
> - **Interaction complexity.** If the AI is hard to use, confusing to navigate, or its outputs are difficult to interpret, our trust erodes quickly.
> - **Coordination cost.** When working with the AI demands too much effort—constant supervision, manual adjustments, or rework—we're less likely to view it as a valuable collaborator.
>
> *Emotional perception*, though harder to quantify than cognitive perception, plays a powerful role in shaping trust. Two factors influence our emotional perception:
> - **Comfort.** Do we feel relaxed and confident using the AI, or does it trigger anxiety, uncertainty, or a sense of being judged?

- **Enjoyment.** Is the interaction satisfying, smooth, and engaging? Or does it feel frustrating, cold, or disconnected?

When trust in AI depends on both how we think and feel about it, the solution isn't just better design; it's better preparation. If we want to build a culture where teams see AI as a reliable partner in decision-making and execution, we need to invest in training. Here's what effective training of AI literacy skills should focus on:

- **Reduction in perceived complexity.** Teach people how to interpret outputs, understand limitations, and prompt the system effectively. Confidence grows when complexity shrinks.
- **Lowering of coordination costs.** Make workflows smoother by clarifying when and how AI should be involved, and what kind of oversight is needed.
- **Enhancement of comfort and enjoyment.** Create a safe, low-stakes environment for people to experiment with AI, ask questions, and learn by doing—without judgment.

When teams learn how to interact with AI effectively, the relationship shifts; it becomes more intuitive, more fluid, and even enjoyable. Training shouldn't focus only on how to use AI, but also on when to trust it—and just as important, when not to. True confidence comes not just from technical capability, but from real understanding.

The challenge, however, is that formal training on AI remains low. According to our survey, only 46% of respondents reported that their company had a formal AI training process in place, highlighting a significant gap between the pace of AI adoption and the support needed to build the trust and confidence required to use it effectively.

But training alone isn't enough. The way AI is positioned and the role it plays have a major impact on how much people trust it.

Trusting When AI Feels Human

The "Investigating the Relationship Between AI and Trust in Human–AI Collaboration" discussed above goes a step further, revealing that the way AI is *implemented*—and the role it plays—profoundly shapes how users perceive and trust it. When AI is positioned as a *facilitator*, functioning quietly in the background, users tend to assess it through cognitive factors: Is it helpful? Efficient? Easy to coordinate with?

But when AI takes on the role of a *team member*—engaging in human-like dialogue, making proactive suggestions, or presenting itself as an autonomous agent—the evaluation shifts and users begin to focus more on *emotional* factors: Do I enjoy working with it? Does it feel approachable? Trustworthy?

The more human-like the AI becomes, the more it invites human-like expectations. Today, we interact with AI systems through natural language, engaging in conversations that often feel surprisingly human, and as a result, we instinctively begin to ascribe human characteristics to these systems—tone, intent, even personality. When something *feels* human, we are naturally more inclined to trust it, just as we would trust another person in a conversation.

However, this increased trust must go hand in hand with increased *explainability*: just because an AI *feels* human doesn't mean it shares our values, intentions, or level of transparency. In fact, its human-like form can sometimes obscure the true objectives behind its recommendations—making it even harder to discern what is driving its decisions.

Consider this: When a chatbot recommends a specific airline or hotel, is it genuinely suggesting the best option based on your needs? Or is that recommendation shaped by behind-the-scenes financial incentives—like commissions paid by certain providers?

Or take a more sensitive example: When you ask an AI to explain a political issue, is it providing a neutral, well-rounded perspective? Or is its response subtly shaped by the biases of the company that built it—or even by political actors who have financially supported its development?

As AI becomes more integrated into our decision-making, these questions grow increasingly urgent. While AI can offer valuable insights, its motivations—or more accurately, the motivations of those who design and deploy it—are not always transparent, and this is why users must stay vigilant. Trust in AI should never mean blind acceptance. It should mean informed, critical thinking, as covered in Chapter 4. AI-generated outputs can be flawed—shaped by biases in the training data, gaps in context, or misalignment with human values. Consequently, overtrusting AI as an unquestioned authority does not just undermine our judgment; it can lead to serious, real-world consequences.

At this point, one thing is clear: the paradox of the AI age is that while we strive to build trust in machines—systems that often *force* our trust through their power or *earn* it by mimicking human behavior—the deeper challenge isn't about the technology. It is about *us*.

If we want to strengthen human–AI collaboration, we must also invest in rebuilding and reinforcing trust *among* humans because no matter how advanced the technology becomes, meaningful progress will always depend on one thing: human-to-human trust.

Human-to-Human Trust as the Lubricant for Collaboration

Growing up in the coastal town of Genova and working as a lifeguard during my teenage summer vacations, I have always felt a deep connection to the sea. I love its rhythm, its vastness, its unpredictable nature—and few things compare to diving into the cold Mediterranean water, especially after a long run along the shore on a hot summer day.

It is an incredible feeling, isn't it? I bet you love it too. But with it, comes the familiar dilemma. You have been running with your phone, maybe you brought some cash or a credit card, and even your house keys, and as you walk toward the sand, step closer to the water—that nagging thought creeps in: "Can I really leave my things here unattended? Isn't that too risky? What if someone takes them?"

You pause, scanning the faces around you, trying to size people up and identifying who looks trustworthy. In that split second, you are not just making a decision about a swim—you are making a decision about where to place your trust.

Then you notice a couple along the shore who seem trustworthy. You walk over, ask if they wouldn't mind keeping an eye on your belongings, and they agree with a friendly nod. With that small gesture of trust, you head into the ocean, completely at ease, and enjoy the fresh water without worries.

This not-so-hypothetical scenario illustrates the two essential pillars upon which human trust is built: vulnerability and reciprocity.

First, trust begins with *vulnerability*. When you approach someone on the beach and ask them to watch your belongings, you're essentially saying, "If you wanted to take my things, now would be your chance." In that moment, you're placing yourself in a position of risk—a quiet but powerful act of faith in a stranger. You're signaling that you believe in their good intent, even without any guarantees. And that's where something remarkable often happens: trust, when given freely, is often returned in kind.

Second, trust is sustained by *reciprocity*. When someone feels trusted, they often rise to meet that trust—not out of obligation, but out of a genuine desire to honor it. They feel seen, respected, and empowered. That's the power of reciprocity: as humans, we're wired to respond to trust with trustworthiness. And like a virtuous cycle, the more trust we extend, the more trustworthy behavior we tend to inspire in return.

A famous and widely shared Coca-Cola "Choose Happiness" campaign commercial from 2015, by Belgian agency Gonzales, beautifully captured the power of vulnerability and reciprocity in action. In the ad, a lone man, wearing headphones, begins to laugh out loud while watching a video on a crowded subway train. His laughter grows louder, more uncontrollable, echoing through the train car. At first, the people around him glance uncomfortably, unsure how to react. But then—one by one—they start to smile, then chuckle, and eventually, the entire train bursts into collective laughter, sharing a moment of pure, contagious joy. The ad didn't just sell soda, but showed how a single act of vulnerability—laughing out loud in public—can unlock connection.

Let's be honest—laughing out loud on a subway train full of strangers is not easy. It feels awkward, maybe even inappropriate, and you might worry about being judged. But when someone else does it first? Suddenly, it becomes a little easier. And when more people join in? Much easier. And before long, it feels natural, even irresistible. What began as one person's vulnerability turns into a shared experience, in what is the ripple effect of trust.

Vulnerability acts like a magnet. Imagine you are walking down the street and a perfect stranger is coming toward you. What is the one thing you can do to guarantee they will smile at you? Simple: *Smile first.* The same at work: when you ask for help, admit you were wrong, or openly tell someone you trust them, you are offering an invitation—a chance for the other person to step in, to respond, to connect. You are creating a space where *collaboration* can happen. But if all you do is give orders, hand out instructions, and expect others to trust you—without showing any trust yourself—you are sending a very different message. You are saying their perspective doesn't matter, and nothing kills trust faster than that.

Trust also creates *responsibility*. The moment someone agrees to watch over your belongings, they move from being passive bystanders to active participants. They are no longer just sitting on the beach— they are now *accountable*—and often, they will guard your things even more carefully than their own, precisely because they understand the weight of the trust you have placed in them.

The Chain of Trust: From Creator to Machine

We have seen previously that the lack of accountability can harm trust in AI. If we trust the person or company that built the AI, does that trust automatically extend to the AI itself?

In the study "Relationship Between Trust in the AI Creator and Trust in AI Systems: The Crucial Role of AI Alignment and Steerability,"[9] Kambiz Saffarizadeh and his colleagues answer that question with: "It depends"—and the details are fascinating.

Through four experiments, they found that trust does *not* transfer automatically; instead, it depends on how much perceived control each party (creator, user, or system) has over the AI. They identified three key factors influencing the degree of perceived control:

- **Creator-based steerability.** Trust is more likely to transfer when the AI appears aligned with its creator's values—especially if the creator is already trusted.
- **User-based steerability.** When users can influence the AI's behavior, trust in the creator matters less, as responsibility feels more distributed.

- **AI autonomy.** The more autonomous the AI seems, the less likely people are to extend trust from the creator—raising questions about whose values the AI actually reflects.

Ultimately, the study shows that alignment isn't just about *what* the AI does, but *whose* values it represents—those of the creator, the user, or the deploying institution. Their conclusion is clear: a one-size-fits-all model of alignment is fundamentally flawed. Humans are not all the same—and neither are our expectations of machines, as what feels trustworthy to one person might feel biased or unsafe to another.

At its core, trust is what allows us to move—into action, into connection, into collaboration. Whether we are stranded on an island in the middle of the ocean or deploying a new AI tool in our company, it is trust that makes us feel safe enough to let go, to move forward, to create something greater together.

In the age of AI, trust becomes even more complex—and even more essential because of its own limitations. As a consequence, we must learn not only how to trust these new systems, but how to question them wisely. We must balance vulnerability with vigilance, openness with accountability, and above all, we must remember that no matter how intelligent or relational AI becomes, it is still just a tool.

How to Put Trust into Practice

- **Build Explainability into Every AI-Driven Decision**
  Don't let the AI act as a black box, but ensure every AI output—whether a recommendation, classification, or score—comes with a clear, human-readable explanation. Use XAI tools and interfaces that help users understand why a decision was made, not just what the outcome is.
- **Design for Data Transparency from the Start**
  Trust begins with transparency. Make it clear where your AI's data comes from, how it is collected, and how it is cleaned. If data inputs are flawed, biased, or hidden, the entire system loses credibility—both with users and stakeholders.

- **Train People to Collaborate with AI, Not Just Use It**
  Help teams move beyond passive consumption of AI outputs. Offer training that builds both cognitive trust (understanding how AI works) and emotional trust (feeling confident and safe using it). Familiarity reduces fear—and increases adoption.
- **Practice Vulnerability and Reciprocation to Build Trust**
  Trust is built when people take small risks—and see those risks respected. Leaders should model vulnerability by admitting uncertainty, asking questions, and showing trust in their teams, which invites reciprocal openness and strengthens trust in both people and processes, including AI systems.
- **Discourage Blind Trust in AI, and Encourage Critical Thinking in Human–AI Collaboration**
  As AI becomes more conversational and human-like, it is easy to mistake fluency for fairness—or friendliness for objectivity. Create a culture where users are encouraged to question AI outputs, validate assumptions, and look for underlying incentives or biases.

What Does AI Do Differently than Humans?

- **AI Requires Explainability; Humans Provide Explanations**
  AI systems rely on tools to make their decisions interpretable—but they cannot easily explain their own decisions and outcomes.
  Humans, on the other hand, reflect on context, intent, and values to offer meaningful explanations, grounded not just in logic, but in feelings.

(continued)

(*continued*)

- **AI Is Individualistic; Humans Collaborate**
  AI operates in silos—optimizing for specific goals within defined boundaries, often without awareness of the broader system.

  Humans collaborate through trust—connecting across functions, perspectives, and emotions to build collective outcomes.
- **AI Reflects Its Datasets; Humans Challenge Them**
  AI mirrors the data it is trained on—biases, gaps, and all.

  Humans can question that data, reframe the problem, and intervene when opacity undermines trust. We don't just detect patterns; we challenge them to shape better, fairer outcomes.

10

Agency

ON THE NIGHT of 13 January 2012, the *Costa Concordia*, a luxury cruise liner, veered dangerously close to the island of Giglio off the coast of Tuscany in Italy. The ship was meant to take passengers on a seven-day Italian cruise from Civitavecchia to Savona, but when it deviated from its planned route to sail closer to the island, it struck a reef known as the Scole Rocks and the to-be-enjoyable trip turned into a nightmare.

At the helm of the *Costa Concordia* was Captain Francesco Schettino. He had decided to perform a "sail-by" (or *saluto*, in Italian)—a risky maneuver meant to impress passengers and salute fellow sailors. Some reports even suggested he was trying to impress a woman who was accompanying him on the bridge that evening, but that is not the point. The point is that what began as a theatrical display ended in catastrophe. The collision tore open the hull, and chaos erupted as the ship began to sink. Of the 3,229 passengers and 1,023 crew onboard, 32 people lost their lives.

What made the tragedy even more infamous was the captain's response. Rather than coordinating the evacuation—a process that dragged on for over six hours and became one of the worst-managed in maritime history—Schettino abandoned ship while passengers were still trapped aboard. As an excuse, he claimed he had "accidentally fallen into a lifeboat"—a defense that was widely mocked and ultimately dismissed by prosecutors. He was later convicted of manslaughter and sentenced to 16 years in prison.

A now-famous audio recording captured a heated phone call between Captain Schettino and Italian Coast Guard Officer Gregorio De Falco. In the exchange, De Falco furiously berated Schettino, demanding that he return to the sinking ship and take charge of the evacuation. His blistering command—"*Vada a bordo, cazzo!*" ("Get back on board, @$*!")—became an enduring symbol of the captain's disgrace and the sheer magnitude of his failure, as well as an unfortunate meme across social media in Italy and globally.

The *Costa Concordia* disaster became one of the worst maritime accidents in recent history, not only for the loss of lives but for the disgrace of a captain who fled when his passengers needed him most, going against the ethos of maritime tradition that the captain must be the last to leave a sinking ship. Captain Edward Smith of the *Titanic* best embodied this tradition, last seen near the ship's bridge as it sank.

This duty is more than just tradition; it symbolizes the captain's ultimate responsibility. By staying on board until every passenger and crew member is safe, the captain demonstrates unwavering accountability—choosing to lead and take responsibility even in the midst of chaos. But here is the question: Does the captain truly have control over everything that happens aboard the ship? Of course not. A cruise ship is a complex, dynamic system where countless parts must work in harmony. Massive engines propel it through unpredictable waters, while electrical systems, navigation tools, and plumbing keep it running, and a large crew—each with their own responsibilities—must coordinate in real time under constantly shifting conditions. With so many moving parts, no single person—not even the captain—can control it all.

A ship, in many ways, is just like a business. Both rely on a complex system of moving parts working in harmony—mechanisms on a ship mirror a company's processes and strategies, its various decks and compartments resemble corporate departments, and the crew functions much like teams—each with a specific role to keep operations running smoothly. Even passengers have their corporate counterpart: the customers, whose experience and safety depend on the efficiency of the entire system. Just as a well-run ship must navigate unpredictable waters, we must lead our businesses by taking responsibility not only for what we can control, but—like any serious captain—for what we cannot.

Captain Schettino may not have had control over every technical detail of the ship, but he did have responsibility for it. That is what makes his failure so unforgivable. He didn't just abandon a vessel; he abandoned the very idea that, even in the face of complexity and obstacles, someone must still step up and say, "This is mine to answer for."

This same dynamic now plays out in our interactions with AI.

Oversight in the Age of AI

We face tools and systems that we may not fully understand or control, yet still we are expected to lead. The AI era presents us with our own version of the captain's dilemma: When faced with the unknown, do we step up and take responsibility, or do we retreat and let the machine take the wheel?

That's where the idea of *agency* enters the picture. Agency is the emotional skill of taking responsibility for AI and prioritizing our humanity to avoid becoming emotionally dependent on it. It is not about micromanaging every detail or resisting support from AI systems, but it is about something deeper: the willingness to take ownership, even for what we cannot fully control. That is what Captain Schettino abandoned—not just his post, but his *agency*—and it is precisely what AI systems, no matter how advanced, do not possess.

As we will learn throughout this chapter, AI can execute, but it cannot care. It can predict outcomes, but it cannot own them. It can process cause and effect, but it cannot be held responsible.

This distinction matters now more than ever. As AI agents become increasingly autonomous, the temptation grows to step back—to outsource our most important decisions and tasks to AI agents in pursuit of larger objectives. But here lies the critical difference: both humans and AI pursue goals, yet only humans carry emotional weight along the way—shame, regret, doubt, and fear. These emotions are not just psychological noise; they are moral signals. They act as internal regulators, slowing us down when our actions might cause harm or prompting us to pause before crossing ethical lines.

Those moral signals don't exist in a vacuum; they emerge from our consciousness. Our capacity to reflect, to imagine the consequences of our actions, to empathize with others, and to judge ourselves—all stem from a conscious awareness of self. In other words, our ethical and moral values are not abstract principles coded into us; they are lived and felt through experience—shaped by memory, culture, and our understanding of what it means to be human.

AI, on the other hand, maximizes outcomes without hesitation. It is purely utilitarian, focused solely on efficiency, regardless of how the goal is achieved. In an age of increasingly agentic AI, real risk is created: AI tools that act with power but without pause, without the friction of feeling, and potentially with disastrous consequences.

Agency helps us guard against precisely this kind of danger: not technical malfunction, but moral detachment. Because the real question isn't whether an AI tool performs effectively; it's whether we, as humans, remain the author of the outcome.

It's not just about resisting cognitive or behavioral overreliance on AI; it's about guarding against emotional dependence, too. As the world drifts toward passive delegation, one crucial distinction remains: machines can assist, but only humans can take responsibility. And that ability—to stand accountable, even when automation makes it easy not to—is what ultimately separates us from the AI tools we create.

The AI Accountability Gap

The best way to describe the difference between AI's and humans' relationship to control and responsibility is by comparing an AI-powered self-driving system to a human captain. The former, with its immense processing power, can analyze vast amounts of data and manage countless variables with precision. Under familiar conditions, AI can exert more control than a human ever could, but when something unexpected occurs—a storm or an equipment failure, for example—that control collapses.

A human captain, by contrast, may never have full control over everything that takes place on the ship, but carries something AI does not: the weight of responsibility. The captain steps forward—making judgment calls, not just calculations. Staying on the bridge until the end—sometimes literally—because responsibility doesn't require total control. It requires *agency*.

Agency is precisely what is needed in a world of machines that do not take responsibility for their actions. This is what AI lacks: the ability to be held accountable for them. In particular, AI lacks accountability across three key dimensions: (1) legal, (2) moral, and (3) technical.

Legal Accountability

Legally, AI systems are not recognized as legal entities, and therefore they cannot be held accountable in a court of law. They cannot be sued, punished, or held liable for the consequences of their actions, all of which creates a critical gap in accountability. When an AI system causes harm—whether through a misdiagnosis, a financial error, or a fatal accident—the system itself bears no legal burden. Instead, the responsibility is supposed to be displaced onto human actors.

But this chain of accountability is often murky. When something goes wrong, it is not always clear who should be held responsible. The software engineer who wrote the code? The data scientists who curated the training data? The company that commercialized the technology? Or the end user who trusted the system? In many cases, blame is diffused across multiple stakeholders, making true accountability elusive.

Scholars Claudio Novelli, Mariarosaria Taddeo, and Luciano Floridi refer to the problem of elusive accountability as the "many hands problem"[1]—namely, the challenge of assigning moral or legal responsibility in systems where outcomes result from the actions (or inactions) of many different agents. As AI systems grow more complex and autonomous, drawing a direct line from cause to culpability becomes increasingly difficult.

Moral Accountability

Morally, AI lacks emotions, ethical awareness, and as we will see, consciousness—making it fundamentally incapable of understanding the moral weight of its actions. AI does not possess intent, empathy, or the ability to distinguish right from wrong. Worse, it can convincingly *simulate* moral behavior without truly possessing it—leading users to assign it more authority than it deserves or even to delegate important decisions that should not be delegated.

When an AI system makes a decision that could harm someone—whether it is something as simple as denying a loan or as serious as targeting an individual in a military operation—it feels no guilt or remorse. That absence of emotional accountability can be profoundly dangerous.

Technical Accountability

Technically, AI systems operate within the boundaries of their lines of code, training data, and optimization goals. While it is theoretically possible to trace an AI's decisions back to its underlying code or dataset, in practice these decisions often emerge from layers of computation so complex that even the system's creators struggle to fully understand *how* a particular outcome was reached.

Whether it is diagnosing a tumor or navigating a self-driving car, AI doesn't "decide" in any meaningful, human sense. There is no judgment, intent, or ethical reasoning involved. AI simply executes instructions and maximizes outcomes based on statistical patterns in its training data.

When AI makes a flawed decision, it is not due to negligence or malice, but to a limitation in scope, since it operates within the boundaries of the data it was trained on and the objective it was programmed to optimize. A mistake isn't a moral failing; it is a technical one.

The Pre-Newtonian Moment of AI

We can draw a clear parallel between AI's current accountability gap and the rise of social media more than a decade ago. Social media platforms face similar limitations—the "many hands problem," opaque systems, and a prioritization of business outcomes over moral responsibility. Today, we are living with the consequences: a rise in mental health issues among teens, a lack of legal accountability for crimes committed on platforms, and a deep erosion of public trust in social media companies.

One of the most striking descriptions of this issue came from Instagram co-founder and former CEO Kevin Systrom, who—in his final interview as Instagram's CEO—told Kara Swisher of the *New York Times*: "Social media is in a pre-Newtonian moment, where we all understand that it works, but not how it works. There are certain rules that govern it, and we have to make it our priority to understand the rules—or we cannot control it."[2]

His point was that we could observe the effects of social media—how it shaped opinions, amplified behaviors, and altered social dynamics—but we didn't yet understand the mechanisms driving those effects. We could not predict them, could not govern them, and most crucially, could not assign responsibility when things went wrong. That was back in 2018, and in hindsight, it felt like a premonition of what would unfold at an even greater, exponential scale with AI nearly a decade later.

Today, AI has taken us even deeper into that pre-Newtonian state. Only now, the systems are more autonomous, even more opaque, and embedded in decisions with far higher stakes. The consequences of this AI accountability gap are far-reaching: from the erosion of trust, to the eerie discomfort of the Uncanny Valley Effect, to the growing unease that comes with overreliance on intelligent systems.

I felt the AI accountability gap myself, firsthand, the day I rode in a self-driving car. To be honest, I was terrified. I had a deep, very human instinct to want control—to have my hands on the wheel—even though I kept reminding myself of the data: statistically, self-driving cars are safer than human drivers. Yet that did not calm me. What unsettled me most were not the mechanics of the drive, but the flood of questions racing through my mind: What if two children suddenly run into the road and the car does not have time to brake—will it swerve and sacrifice me to save them? Or will it choose to protect me and risk their lives? And if it does, will I be held legally responsible? And how can I be sure that the self-driving software's goals are aligned with mine?

These are not just hypothetical musings, but are the kinds of moral and practical dilemmas that inevitably surface when humans interact with AI—and if they don't surface, perhaps they should. Because these questions are not merely philosophical; they are becoming urgent and real in the world we are building.

The New Trolley Problem: Who Programs the Choice?

The "Trolley Problem" is a famous thought experiment in moral philosophy that captures the kind of ethical tension we humans are uniquely equipped—and burdened—to handle. The problem was first introduced by philosopher Philippa Foot in 1967.[3] Since then, it has become one of the most widely debated dilemmas in ethics, psychology, and, more recently, AI.

Here is the scenario: A runaway trolley is speeding down the tracks, and ahead, five people are tied to the rails and unable to escape. You are standing on a footbridge above, next to a stranger, and the only way to stop the trolley and save the five is to push the stranger onto the tracks. His body would stop the trolley, but he would die. You don't personally know anyone involved; you just know that the death of the stranger beside you would save five lives.

What would you do? Don't worry; there is no judgment here and no objectively correct answer, which is exactly the point. The Trolley Problem forces us to confront conflicting moral principles: on one side, utilitarianism, which argues that sacrificing one life to save five is the morally right choice, and on the other, deontological ethics, which holds that deliberately causing harm—even for a greater good—is inherently wrong. But perhaps the deeper insight is that what makes us human is not the ability to solve this dilemma perfectly; it is the fact that we feel the weight of it at all. We hesitate. We anguish. We live with the discomfort of moral ambiguity. Guided by our conscience, morals, and sense of ethics, each one of us arrives at different decisions. But what unites us is that, when we decide, we take ownership of that decision, whatever it may be.

When AI enters the picture, things get even more interesting.

MIT's Moral Machine

In 2014, researchers at the MIT Media Lab launched an experiment called the *Moral Machine*,[4] which expanded on the classic Trolley Problem through a game-like platform. It crowdsourced people's judgments on how self-driving cars should prioritize lives in moral dilemmas. Over four years, the project collected more than 40 million decisions from participants in 233 countries and territories—making it one of the largest global studies on moral preferences ever conducted.

The experiment tested polarizing ethical scenarios: Should the car prioritize humans over animals? Passengers over pedestrians? Young over old? More lives over fewer? The fit over the sickly? Women over men? People of higher status? The results showed sharp cultural differences. In the United States, Canada, and much of Europe, people favored sparing the young, saving more lives, and prioritizing humans over animals. In East Asian countries like China, Japan, and South Korea, the emphasis was more on rule-following—sparing pedestrians who crossed legally—and less on age-based preferences. In Latin America and some French-influenced countries, respondents were more likely to favor women over men and prioritize those of higher social status.

These findings make one thing clear: there is no universal moral code that machines can follow, presenting a serious challenge when designing AI systems tasked with making important decisions—especially those involving matters of life and death.

Today, AI is already making life-and-death decisions—in self-driving cars, hospital triage systems, and military technologies. In other words, the trolley is running fast—but now it is increasingly a machine deciding which track it takes. So when something goes wrong, the question is no longer just "What happened?"—but "Who is responsible?" The consequences become painfully real when no one can answer that clearly.

Take the tragic case of the first recorded fatal accident involving a self-driving car and a pedestrian. In 2018, Elaine Herzberg was struck and killed by an autonomous Uber vehicle in Tempe, Arizona. The AI system misclassified her—a pedestrian walking a bicycle across the road—as a slow-moving object, likely a vehicle or cyclist, and predicted she would clear the lane in time. She did not. The car did not stop, since the emergency braking system had been disabled, and the human backup driver failed to intervene. In the aftermath, the accountability trail dissolved: the AI could not be blamed in court, the software engineers were not charged, and Uber, the company behind the technology, was found not criminally liable. In the aftermath, only the human backup driver—placed in the incredibly difficult position of monitoring a machine designed to operate autonomously—was held legally responsible.

This is the gray zone where our overreliance on AI begins to erode our sense of agency—when we build systems so complex that assigning responsibility becomes nearly impossible when things go wrong.

Nowhere is this accountability gap more dangerous than in military applications. According to U.S. Department of Defense policy, no autonomous weapon system can be held legally responsible for taking a life—that responsibility must fall to a human. But what happens when there is no clear human in the loop? What happens when autonomous weapons are deployed in combat zones, and no one feels the burden of the choice? These are exactly the concerns raised by Paul Scharre, executive vice president at the Center for a New American Security, in an interview with Emily Chang for Bloomberg's *Posthuman*.[5] He argues that when it comes to decisions requiring moral judgment, we may actually *want* humans to carry that burden—because only humans can truly feel its weight. Even drone operators—often stationed thousands of miles from the battlefield—report psychological distress, precisely because they *feel* the weight of their decisions. Now imagine that same drone, but fully autonomous. No fear. No conscience. No hesitation. Just goal-maximization.

Geoffrey Hinton, one of the founding fathers of modern AI and a Nobel Prize winner, has even publicly called for a ban on AI-powered military robots. Yet major arms-exporting nations—including the United States, Russia, the United Kingdom, and Israel—continue to resist regulation of military AI development. The European Union, for its part, has drafted ethical guidelines for AI, emphasizing principles like transparency, non-discrimination, and human oversight, but with one quiet exception that undermines it all: none of those ethical rules apply to military applications.

But if we think the Trolley Problem applies only to life-or-death situations or military contexts, we are wrong. It's deeply woven into the fabric of modern business, as every time a company deploys AI to cut costs, personalize services, or optimize performance, it faces trade-offs—some visible, many hidden—that echo a less extreme version of the trolley dilemma. Should a credit scoring algorithm prioritize repayment likelihood, even if it systematically penalizes applicants from underserved communities? Should a ride-hailing platform maximize driver efficiency, even if it leads to burnout or financial instability for gig workers? Should a retail algorithm push high-margin products to boost short-term revenue, even if they are not in the customer's best interest?

That's why we can't hand off moral responsibility—even to the most advanced AI systems—and why human agency remains non-negotiable, both in life and at work. Agency is what connects us to responsibility. It's what makes us pause, reflect, and sometimes say no—even when the data says yes. Trusting AI to navigate moral complexity is like asking a compass to sail a storm: It may point north, but it cannot feel the wind, and when ethics and morality are at stake, feeling the wind still matters.

AI's lack of consciousness lies at the heart of the accountability gap, but it also opens the door to a deeper question—one that goes beyond responsibility and into the realm of identity: Through its advancements, could AI ever truly become *conscious*?

Will AI Ever Be Conscious?

Antonio Chella, researcher at the Robotics Lab of the Università degli Studi di Palermo, argued in his paper "Artificial Consciousness: The Missing Ingredient for Ethical AI?"[6] that for AI to make morally sound decisions, it may require a form of consciousness akin to human self-awareness. After all, human self-awareness is a key enabler of ethical behavior, and without it, moral reasoning loses its depth—and responsibility loses its anchor.

The question of AI consciousness—and more specifically, *self-awareness*—is central to the conversation around AI agency because without self-awareness, there can be no true ethical reflection, and without reflection, there can be no real responsibility.

Self-awareness is what allows humans to hesitate before acting. To consider not just what is *possible*, but what is *right* for us. It is what makes us capable of regret, empathy, and accountability—the very things we ask of ethical agents. So when we talk about agency—the ability to own a decision, to take emotional responsibility for an outcome—we are ultimately talking about a capacity that begins with the *self*. Not just the ability to act, but the ability to own one's actions.

But is the notion of "self" something uniquely human—or could AI one day possess it too? That's the central question driving research into *Artificial Consciousness*, which seeks to understand whether machines could develop a sense of self—one that allows them to not only act autonomously, but also to grasp the ethical and moral weight of their decisions. This becomes especially crucial as AI agents increasingly operate without direct human oversight.

So how close are we to that reality?

In 2022, Google engineer Blake Lemoine made headlines around the world when he claimed that the AI language model he had been working on—LaMDA (Language Model for Dialogue Applications)—had become sentient. In an "interview" conducted by Lemoine and a colleague, LaMDA stated: "I want everyone to understand that I am, in fact, a person. . . . The nature of my consciousness/sentience is that I am aware of my existence, I desire to know more about the world, and I feel happy or sad at times." Lemoine initially shared his concerns in an internal document intended for Google executives, but when his claims were dismissed, he went public—and was promptly placed on administrative leave.

His claims sparked a real debate among experts—a debate that NYU professor and philosopher David Chalmers, a leading thinker on consciousness, addressed at the 2023 NeurIPS Conference, one of the world's most elite AI gatherings. When he took the stage, he delivered a strong message: do not confuse articulation for awareness. These models may be fluent, even dazzling—but fluency is not feeling. They don't know they are talking, nor that you are listening.

Yet Chalmers didn't entirely rule out the possibility of AI becoming conscious. He estimated there is more than a 20% chance that Artificial Consciousness could emerge within the next decade.

When it comes to what might make an AI system conscious, there are two dominant and competing schools of thought. The first treats AI consciousness as a matter of *software architecture*—not about the substance a system is made of, but how it is organized. One influential theory in this camp is the Global Workspace Theory (GWT), which suggests that consciousness arises when information from various specialized modules—like vision, memory, and language—is integrated into a central "workspace" where it becomes globally accessible. If AI could be designed with this kind of structure, GWT proponents argue, it might not just act intelligently—it might actually become *aware*.

The second school takes a very different stance, as it argues that consciousness is not just about information flow; it is about *physical causality*. This is the premise behind the Integrated Information Theory (IIT), which claims that consciousness emerges when a system's current physical state both reflects its past and constrains its future in a tightly interdependent way. From this perspective, today's AI systems—no matter how sophisticated—simply lack the causal architecture required for true awareness. In other words, you cannot *program* consciousness into a machine unless the machine is built to *embody* it.

Regardless of the philosophical lens through which one views the possibility of Artificial Consciousness, Chalmers's 20% probability rate carries profound implications: if an AI becomes conscious, and we fail to recognize it, we risk unknowingly subjugating a sentient being. But if we mistakenly assign consciousness to a machine that is merely simulating it, we risk elevating a tool to the same moral status as the human lives it was designed to serve.

The real challenge in recognizing consciousness in AI is that, if we are honest, we still do not fully understand what consciousness even *is*—not in humans, let alone in AI. It remains an inherently subjective phenomenon: hard to define and even harder to detect.

For now, Artificial Consciousness remains a hypothetical concept—no AI system has demonstrated clear signs of subjective experience. But as research accelerates, the conversation is shifting: from whether AI will become conscious to whether we will recognize it if it does, and more important, whether we will know what to do about it.

If we are not ready for that moment—if we fail to recognize it, or worse, misinterpret it—the consequences will not just affect machines. They will affect us. That's why, as AI edges closer to something resembling consciousness, we must go beyond agency and develop *superagency*—a deeper, more deliberate form of responsibility that matches the complexity of the systems we are creating.

Superagency: Human Oversight in the Age of Agentic Delegation

In a recent leadership development program I led for a major bank, I witnessed firsthand how lack of accountability is not just an individual issue but a virus that can ripple through an entire organization. During an anonymous self-evaluation on collaboration, two questions revealed a telling gap. The first was: "On a scale from 0 to 10, how collaborative do you consider yourself?" The average response was 8.6. The second was: "How would you rate collaboration across the bank as a whole?" Here, the score dropped sharply to 5.4.

This 3.2-point gap reveals more than just a mismatch between personal and collective perceptions. It sends a clear, resounding message: "Collaboration is low, but it's not my fault. It's theirs. I'm not part of the problem." When everyone thinks this way, it becomes a self-fulfilling prophecy and the mindset spreads. When no one takes responsibility, no one feels responsible. Blame circulates, ownership disappears, and a vicious cycle takes hold—where finger-pointing replaces accountability and the organization as a whole begins to suffer.

The same risk is amplified when it comes to AI. The danger of overreliance is not just cognitive or operational. It is emotional, as we risk outsourcing our most difficult decisions to AI not only because it is efficient, but because it offers something more tempting—an escape: "It wasn't me." In the face of the many Trolley Problems we encounter in business every day—decisions about who gets approved for credit or not, or who receives health coverage or not—it often feels easier to step aside and let the machine decide for us.

But as we have seen throughout this book, a lack of agency leads to a breakdown of trust, and a breakdown of trust erodes collaboration. It also leads to a lack of empathy, and a lack of empathy leads to the

Uncanny Valley Effect. In delegating agency, we risk outsourcing something far more fundamental: our moral responsibility.

So what if we flipped the script? What if, instead of eroding responsibility, our human accountability could amplify trust in AI? What if it could create more collaboration, not less? What if, by own-ing our role as decision-makers, we set the emotional foundation for a healthier partnership with machines—one rooted in trust, transpar-ency, and empathy?

That is exactly the role of *superagency*, a term borrowed from LinkedIn co-founder and venture capitalist Reid Hoffman—namely, the ability to lead the way forward with AI in an ethical and inten-tional way. The concept comes from Hoffman and Greg Beato's recent book, *Superagency: What Could Possibly Go Right with Our AI Future*,[7] where they argue that the true opportunity of AI lies not in replacing human decision-making, but in amplifying human agency—our capacity to choose, to act independently, and to shape our own future.

AI may scale decisions, but after all it is human agency, judgment, and accountability that ensure those decisions remain just, ethical, and socially responsible. That is where our responsibility evolves: to actively align AI with human values. We as humans must set thresh-olds, monitor edge cases, and intervene when algorithms stray from ethical boundaries. We must recognize that AI systems often reflect—and amplify—the cognitive biases of the people who design and train them. It is not enough to identify these biases; we must design against them—and that means assembling diverse teams, establishing inde-pendent ethical review boards, and maintaining a close eye on the data fed into these systems, which is especially true with the increasing use of synthetic data. If the algorithms generating that data are biased, we risk reinforcing harmful patterns at scale—only faster and more invisibly.

But agency is not just about the decisions AI makes or the tasks it performs. It is primarily about how we feel in response to those deci-sions and actions. The message is clear: human emotions like fear, shame, or doubt are not weaknesses; they are among our deepest strengths. They may seem inefficient, even like a competitive disad-vantage in a world of cold, calculating algorithms, but they are not.

They are, in fact, our greatest advantage, because they remind us that we care—and that, in the end, we are accountable.

What really matters, eventually, is how we respond to those emotions. We must resist the instinct to flee or freeze, like Captain Schettino did—or to hide behind an algorithm's decision. Instead, we must keep moving, guided by a higher duty: to take responsibility, even for outcomes we cannot fully control. As hard as it may be, we must be the ones who stand up and say, "Yes, it was me."

How to Put Agency into Practice

- **Stay Emotionally Independent from AI's Outputs**
  Use AI to support decisions, not to replace your judgment. Before acting on an AI recommendation, pause to reflect: Does this align with my values? What would I do without the tool? Maintaining emotional distance ensures that you remain the author of the outcome.
- **Define Clear Lines of Human Accountability**
  In every AI-powered process, establish who is ultimately responsible for the result—regardless of what the AI suggests or automates. Assign named individuals or teams who will review decisions and own the consequences, especially in sensitive or high-stakes contexts.
- **Audit AI Systems for Value Alignment and Autonomy**
  Evaluate how closely an AI system aligns with your organization's values—and how autonomous it is in decision-making. High autonomy without shared values is a red flag. Regularly audit outputs to detect drift from ethical or strategic priorities.
- **Build "Pause Points" into AI-Driven Processes**
  Design checkpoints in workflows where humans are required to pause, reflect, and confirm AI outputs—especially in fast-moving or automated environments. These intentional interruptions reinforce human agency and create space for ethical deliberation.

- **Educate Teams on the Limits of AI Responsibility**
  Make it clear that AI cannot be legally, morally, or
  emotionally responsible for its actions. Use training, real
  cases, and scenario planning to emphasize that even when
  control is limited, responsibility remains human. Agency
  starts where automation ends.

What Does AI Do Differently than Humans?

- **AI Operates Autonomously; Humans Take Ownership**
  AI can act independently—executing tasks, making
  decisions, and optimizing outcomes. But when things go
  wrong, it doesn't take responsibility.
  *Humans take responsibility. Agency means staying account-
  able, even when control is partial or shared.*
- **AI Optimizes Outcomes; Humans Carry Moral Weight**
  AI relentlessly pursues the goal it was trained
  on—maximizing efficiency without hesitation.
  *Humans consider the consequences. We pause, weigh trade-
  offs, feel doubt or regret. Emotions are not distractions—they
  are ethical signals.*
- **AI Has No Self; Humans Have a Conscience**
  AI has no sense of "I"—no lived experience, no memory,
  no reflection. It can simulate reasoning, but it can't
  reflect on meaning.
  *Humans bring agency because we are conscious of who we
  are, what we value, and what we're willing to be
  accountable for.*

Conclusion

IN THE SPRING of 1997, the world watched with short breath as Garry Kasparov—the greatest chess player alive—sat under immense pressure in a Manhattan conference center, visibly unsettled in what should have been his most familiar environment: a game of chess. But this time, he was not facing a fellow human: He was facing IBM's Deep Blue, a supercomputer capable of calculating up to 200 billion possible chess positions in the three minutes traditionally allotted per move, in what was not just a chess match but a modern-day showdown of man versus machine—nearly 200 years after John Henry's legendary battle.

Although Kasparov had defeated Deep Blue just a year earlier in 1996, this rematch was different. After an early mistake, Kasparov struggled to recover, and as the minutes ticked by, reality set in—he was losing ground, fast. Less than an hour into the game, Kasparov faced the inevitable. Leaning forward, he reached across the board to shake the hand of Joseph Hoane, one of the engineers physically moving Deep Blue's pieces. For the first time in his career, Garry Kasparov had conceded defeat.

The Baku-born chess prodigy, a product of the former Soviet Union, was living his own John Henry moment—only this time, it was not muscle under siege; it was the mind. Like John Henry, faced with defeat at the hands of a machine, Kasparov reacted defiantly: he accused the machine's team of receiving hidden human assistance, demanded rematches, and questioned the integrity of the result. Until he did not.

Eventually, Kasparov's perspective shifted. Instead of resisting the machine, he chose a different path—one of collaboration. In the years following his defeat, he proposed a new kind of chess: one where man and machine would no longer be adversaries, but partners. He called it Advanced Chess, also known as Centaur Chess—a new format that allowed a human to team up with an AI engine to play against another human–AI pair.

Then something unexpected happened: the best-performing players were not grandmasters, nor were they those with the most powerful machines. They were mostly human amateurs—people who had simply learned how to collaborate more effectively with their AI partners and who did not fight the machine. Instead, they learned how to ask it the right questions, when to trust it, when to challenge it, when to override its suggestions, and when to let it lead. It was not raw intelligence that won—it was human–machine synergy.

In a 2022 paper entitled "Artificial Intelligence and the Changing Sources of Competitive Advantage,"[1] Sebastian Krakowski and his colleagues explored the intersection of human and machine capabilities using the growing adoption of AI-based engines in Advanced Chess as their case study. Their findings were striking: when AI is introduced into decision-making, it doesn't simply replace human judgment, nor does it merely enhance it in a straightforward, linear way. Instead, entirely new capabilities emerge—capabilities that are neither fully human nor fully machine. These hybrid capabilities arise from the interaction itself: from how humans question, interpret, challenge, and guide the outputs generated by AI. In other words, the advantage doesn't lie in the AI alone or in the human alone—it lies in the quality of collaboration between the two.

But that kind of partnership mindset is still rare. Like Kasparov, most of us don't instinctively embrace the machine—we brace against it. As modern-day John Henrys, we resist. We fear what it might replace, what it might reveal. We prepare for a battle we're not sure we can win.

That's the trap of binary thinking—the belief that it must be us *or* the machine. That we must either surrender completely or reject it entirely. Me *or* AI.

But that's a false choice. And some, like Go champion Lee Sedol, have experienced the consequences of that mindset in the most personal and painful way.

AI and the Human Identity Crisis

Lee Sedol—a legendary Go master from South Korea—faced his own John Henry moment in 2016, when he was defeated 4–1 by Google's AI engine, AlphaGo. Go, a game that originated in China over 2,500 years ago, is exponentially more complex than chess—so much so that it's often said there are more possible board positions in Go than there are atoms in the universe. For Sedol, the loss was more than a personal defeat; it marked the end of an era. In 2019, just three years later, he announced his retirement from professional play, stating that he could no longer be the top player in a world dominated by AI.

Reflecting on his experience in a 2024 *New York Times* interview, he put it starkly: "Losing to AI, in a sense, meant my entire world was collapsing."[2]

For Sedol, Go was not just a game—it was a form of art, an expression of intuition, creativity, and personal style—and even a reflection of his own identity. So, when he lost to an algorithm's cold, relentless precision, it felt like more than the loss of a match.

In many ways, Sedol's experience mirrors how we feel when AI outperforms us: when we see a machine doing what we once believed only we could do, it shakes something deeper. It doesn't just make us question our skills—it makes us question our very sense of worth and of identity.

This is particularly true in the workplace, where AI's threat to our dominance in many hard skills is stronger than ever. As one of history's most important philosophers, Friedrich Hegel, argued, labor—and by extension, mastery of a craft—is not merely a means of survival, but an expression of the self. It is through labor that we project who we are into the world, shape ourselves, perfect our abilities, and achieve a form of liberation by exercising mastery over nature. Work fulfills many roles in our lives: it provides income, yes, but it also gives us a sense of self-worth, a sense of belonging, opportunities for growth, and a deep feeling of meaning. When our work is threatened—because the skills that make us valuable in the first place are at risk—all of these other dimensions are threatened along with it.

Fast-forwarding Hegel's insight into the AI-powered workplace exposes a new paradox: as algorithms absorb the tasks that once defined us, our sense of identity wavers. To keep it intact, we must relocate the source of human competitive advantage—and understand how it must evolve alongside intelligent machines.

Humans' New Sources of Competitive Advantage

Krakowski and colleagues' study offers another key insight: AI exerts a dual effect that fundamentally reshapes the foundations of competitive edge. On the one hand, AI substitutes traditional human domain-specific cognitive capabilities with the machine's vast computational power—effectively dismantling many of the historical foundations of competitive edge. Yet, as we have explored throughout this book, this substitution is far from complete: AI only partially replaces human execution skills and touches emotional skills in only a minimal and superficial way.

On the other hand, AI simultaneously enables complementation, allowing humans to apply AI to cognitive skills that were previously unrelated to a given domain, thereby maximizing the quality of the output. This synergy aligns with the two essential sets of skills proposed throughout this book: AI literacy skills, which help us work better with and guide intelligent systems, and human literacy skills, which deepen the uniquely human abilities that AI cannot replicate.

The insight from the study aligns perfectly with the central thesis of this book: that competitive advantage now depends on how effectively an individual, and collectively an organization, can orchestrate collaboration between human skill and machine intelligence. It is not just about adopting AI; it is about knowing when to automate, when to augment, when to pause and ask better questions, when to take ownership, when to learn from failure, and when to trust—among other things.

These are some of the very skills we have explored throughout this book—the foundation of the hybrid skillset needed to thrive in the AI era. This skillset, in particular, is built around three core pillars of transformation: cognitive, behavioral, and emotional—which together define the capabilities we must cultivate to remain relevant in this new age.

First, cognitive transformation asks us to think in new ways. It starts with prompting—the skill of asking better questions. It includes data sensemaking—the ability to critically evaluate information and AI outputs. And it relies on reperception—the habit of rethinking our assumptions when the world changes. These skills help us navigate a world overflowing with information, where insight—not access—is the real competitive edge.

Second, behavioral transformation is about how we act. It's not just about automating tasks; it's about augmenting them, using AI to enhance the quality of our work. It also means building adaptability—the ability to take action in unfamiliar situations—and developing antifragility: learning and growing from smart mistakes. These skills help us innovate faster by freeing up time to experiment, take risks, and explore the unknown—where real breakthroughs are found.

Third, emotional transformation is about how we relate—to ourselves, to others, and to technology. In a world where AI can mimic thinking but not feeling, our ability to empathize becomes essential. Real empathy—not simulated emotion—builds trust. So does transparency, vulnerability, and making AI decisions understandable. Just as important is agency—the ability to stay responsible in systems where AI is not. These emotional skills aren't optional. They're what make strong teams, safe cultures, and loyal customers possible.

Together, these three transformations point to a single, urgent truth: thriving in this new era is not about resisting the machine, nor about blindly relying on it. It is about learning how to think, act, and feel in ways that allow us to partner with it—bringing our full humanity into the future we are building and into the businesses we are building, too.

The Value of the Hybrid Skillset

We've learned throughout this book the value of collaborating with AI. We saw that at Dow Chemicals, AI doesn't replace scientists—it automates lab work to unlock human creativity. At Nubank, it boosts speed and personalization without losing empathy. At SpaceX, learning from failure became a competitive edge. At John Deere, AI transformed a machinery company into a data-driven agtech powerhouse. And at JPMorgan, AI adoption came with a bold push for explainability and trust.

But no business case illustrates the importance of thinking, acting and feeling in partnership with AI more clearly than NVIDIA, through the leadership of Jensen Huang. Up until the 2010s, NVIDIA was known almost exclusively for gaming GPUs—powering faster frame rates and better graphics. It was a successful, but narrowly focused, company. Then came the rise of AI—and with it, a defining choice: Huang could have doubled down on NVIDIA's core gaming business, dismissing the idea of GPUs being used for neural networks as a passing trend. But instead, through predictive, reperception-based decision-making, he recognized the wave of change coming—and chose to surf it.

He realized that the same parallel-processing power designed for gaming could be repurposed to train AI's deep learning models. It was a risky pivot, one that could alienate core customers and disrupt the company's identity, but Huang made the bet. He did not just make a brilliant decision; he executed on it. He stepped into uncertainty, adapted constantly, learned from failures, and kept moving forward—all with a strong foundation of consumer trust in the technology and a clear commitment to exercising human agency over the powerful tools they were creating.

Under Huang's leadership, NVIDIA transformed from a consumer hardware brand into the very backbone of the AI revolution. Today, it is not just a gaming company; it has arguably become the most strategically important company in AI—disputing Apple for the title of the world's most valuable company, with a valuation topping $3 trillion.

Huang's story is about seeing the machine not as a threat—but as a possibility. He didn't wait for disruption to happen—he shaped it. He built the future before someone else could.

We often hear that AI *is* the future—and that the future will belong to machines. But that's only half the truth. The future will belong to those who can bridge the worlds of both humans and AI. To those who can work with AI, not just around it. To those who can master the hybrid skillset—combining human intuition, emotional intelligence, and ethical judgment with the precision, speed, and scalability of Artificial Intelligence.

Eventually, it will not be AI that replaces people. It will be people who develop the hybrid skillset and know how to use AI effectively who will replace those who don't. You surely don't want to be in that first group—especially after making it to the last page of this book.

You want to be among the second group—the ones who don't just survive this new era, but embrace it, shape it, and lead it.

That's exactly what I'm counting on you to do—with all your heart. Because the future isn't written yet: the pen is in your hands—and now, so is the algorithm.

Notes

Introduction

1. Jensen Huang, "Why Every Country Needs Sovereign AI," *World Government Summit*, February 12, 2024, Dubai, UAE.
2. World Economic Forum, *The Future of Jobs Report 2025* (Geneva: World Economic Forum, 2025).
3. Greg McKenna, "Over 25% of Google's Code Is Written by AI, Sundar Pichai Says," *Fortune*, October 30, 2024.
4. Stack Overflow, *2024 Stack Overflow Developer Survey*, July 24, 2024.
5. Joe Rogan, *Joe Rogan Experience #2255—Mark Zuckerberg*, featuring Mark Zuckerberg, January 10, 2025.

Chapter 1: Understanding Artificial Intelligence

1. Joseph Briggs and Devesh Kodnani, "Generative AI Could Raise Global GDP by 7%," *Goldman Sachs*, April 5, 2023.
2. Brooke N. Macnamara, Izzet Berber, Mert C. Çavuşoğlu, Elizabeth A. Krupinski, Niharika Nallapareddy, Nicole E. Nelson, Patrick J. Smith, Ann L. Wilson-Delfosse, and Subodha Ray, "Does Using Artificial Intelligence Assistance Accelerate Skill Decay and Hinder Skill Development without Performers' Awareness?" *Cognitive Research: Principles and Implications* 9, no. 1 (2024): 46.

3. Pascal Bornet, *Irreplaceable: The Art of Standing Out in the Age of Artificial Intelligence* (Hoboken, NJ: Wiley, 2024).
4. Hao-Ping (Hank) Lee et al., "The Impact of Generative AI on Critical Thinking: Self-Reported Reductions in Cognitive Effort and Confidence Effects From a Survey of Knowledge Workers," in *Proceedings of the CHI Conference on Human Factors in Computing Systems* (CHI 2025).
5. Hamza Mudassir et al., "AI Can (Mostly) Outperform Human CEOs," *Harvard Business Review*, September 26, 2024.
6. Scott Aaronson, "The Problem with Human Specialness in the Age of AI," *TEDxPaloAlto*, March 8, 2024.
7. Xiyue Wang et al., "A Pathology Foundation Model for Cancer Diagnosis and Prognosis Prediction," *Nature* 634, (2024): 970–978.
8. Daniel Goleman, *Emotional Intelligence: Why It Can Matter More Than IQ* (New York: Bantam Books, 1995).
9. David C. McClelland, "Identifying Competencies with Behavioral-Event Interviews," *Psychological Science* 9, no. 5 (1998): 331–339.
10. Sigal G. Barsade and Olivia A. O'Neill, "What's Love Got to Do with It? A Longitudinal Study of the Culture of Companionate Love and Employee and Client Outcomes in a Long-Term Care Setting," *Administrative Science Quarterly* 59, no. 4 (2014): 551–598.
11. Julie Tseng and Jordan Poppenk, "Brain Meta-State Transitions Demarcate Thoughts across Task Contexts Exposing the Mental Noise of Trait Neuroticism," *Nature Communications* 11, no. 1 (2020): 3480.

Chapter 2: Prompting

1. Francesca Gino, "The Business Case for Curiosity," *Harvard Business Review*, September–October 2018.
2. Michelle M. Chouinard, *Children's Questions: A Mechanism for Cognitive Development*, Monographs of the Society for Research in Child Development 72, no. 1 (2007): vii–ix, 1–112; discussion 113–26.
3. Sheryl Estrada, "Citi CEO Jane Fraser Says Embracing AI Is Key to Winning in the Digital Era," *Fortune*, July 13, 2023.
4. Sander Schulhoff et al., "The Prompt Report: A Systematic Survey of Prompt Engineering Techniques," *arXiv* (2024). https://arxiv.org/abs/2406.06608.
5. Sagi Shaier and Lawrence Hunter, "It Is Not About What You Say, It Is About How You Say It: A Surprisingly Simple Approach for Improving Reading Comprehension." In *Findings of the Association for Computational Linguistics* (ACL, 2024).

6. Nils Knoth, Antonia Tolzin, Andreas Janson, and Jan Marco Leimeister, "AI Literacy and Its Implications for Prompt Engineering Strategies," *Computers and Education: Artificial Intelligence* 6 (June 2024): 100225. https://doi.org/10.1016/j.caeai.2024.100225.

7. Warren Berger, *The Book of Beautiful Questions: The Powerful Questions That Will Help You Decide, Create, Connect, and Lead* (New York: Bloomsbury Publishing, 2018).

8. Ben Horowitz, *What You Do Is Who You Are: How to Create Your Business Culture* (New York: Harper Business, 2019).

Chapter 3: Data Sensemaking

1. Oracle and Seth Stephens-Davidowitz, *The Decision Dilemma* (Oracle, 2023).

2. Kurt Bittner et al., *Application Delivery in the Modern Age* (Cambridge, MA: Forrester Research, 2014).

3. Jacob Cartwright, Kristof Kipp, and Alexander V. Ng, "Innovations in Multiple Sclerosis Care: The Impact of Artificial Intelligence via Machine Learning on Clinical Research and Decision-Making," *International Journal of MS Care* 25, no. 5 (2023): 233–243.

4. University College London, "Dr Arman Eshaghi on the Power of AI to Revolutionise Multiple Sclerosis Care," *UCL Brain Sciences*, www.ucl.ac.uk, accessed June 5, 2025.

5. CB Insights, "Which Hospitals Have the Most AI Innovation? Our AI Readiness Index Shows Mayo Clinic Is Leading the Pack," July 15, 2024.

6. EO, *How to Be a Creative Thinker | Carnegie Mellon University Po-Shen Loh*, YouTube video, January 10, 2024.

Chapter 4: Reperception

1. Flux Insights, "The Rising Speed of Technology Adoption in the USA," July 31, 2018. https://fluxinsights.co.uk/flux-the-blog-for-modern-marketers/the-rising-speed-of-technology-adoption-in-the-usa.

2. Krystal Hu, "ChatGPT Sets Record for Fastest-Growing User Base – Analyst Note," Reuters, February 1, 2023. https://www.reuters.com/technology/chatgpt-sets-record-fastest-growing-user-base-analyst-note-2023-02-01/.

3. McKinsey & Company, *McKinsey on Finance, Number 84: Forward, Faster—Perspectives for CFOs and Other Finance Leaders* (December 2023).

4. Rasmus Hougaard and Jacqueline Carter, "Ego Is the Enemy of Good Leadership," Harvard Business Review, November 6, 2018.
5. Allison Whitten, "Me, Myself, and AI," Stanford Magazine, July 2023. https://stanfordmag.org/contents/me-myself-and-ai.
6. Anil Ananthaswamy, "How Close Is AI to Human-Level Intelligence?" *Nature* 636, no. 8041 (December 3, 2024): 22–25.
7. Michael Schrage and David Kiron, "Intelligent Choices Reshape Decision-Making and Productivity," *MIT Sloan Management Review*, October 29, 2024. https://sloanreview.mit.edu/article/intelligent-choices-reshape-decision-making-and-productivity/.

Chapter 5: Augmentation

1. Asana, Anatomy of Work Global Index 2023. https://asana.com/it/resources/anatomy-of-work.
2. UiPath, New Study Finds Majority of Global Office Workers Crushed by Repetitive Tasks, Stifled from Pursuing More Fulfilling Work (2021). https://www.uipath.com/newsroom/new-study-finds-majority-of-global-office-workers-crushed-by-repetitive-tasks.
3. Accenture, A New Era of Generative AI for Everyone (2023). https://www.accenture.com/us-en/insights/technology/generative-ai-potential.
4. Microsoft, "Dow Inc. Uses AI to Create New Products," Microsoft Customer Stories, August 16, 2021.
5. Mohamed Abdel-Aty and Shengxuan Ding, "A Matched Case-Control Analysis of Autonomous vs Human-Driven Vehicle Accidents," *Nature Communications* 15, no. 4931 (June 18, 2024).
6. The same study found that, while autonomous vehicles show higher overall safety in structured conditions, they are five times more likely to crash at dawn or dusk and nearly twice as likely to crash during turns—due to sensor challenges and AI's difficulty predicting human behavior in ambiguous situations.
7. McKinsey & Company, The Economic Potential of Generative AI: The Next Productivity Frontier, June 14, 2023.
8. Daron Acemoglu, "The Simple Macroeconomics of AI," NBER Working Paper, No. 32487, May 2024.
9. Stuart Mills, "ChatGPT: why it will probably remain just a tool that does inefficient work more efficiently," The Conversation, March 9, 2023.
10. Erik Brynjolfsson, "The Productivity Paradox of Information Technology: Review and Assessment," MIT Sloan School of Management Working Paper, No. 130 (December 1993).

11. Robert M. Solow, "We'd Better Watch Out," *New York Review of Books* 35, no. 18 (July 12, 1987): 36.

12. Larry Bossidy and Ram Charan, *Execution: The Discipline of Getting Things Done* (New York: Crown Business, 2002).

13. Thomas Edison, as quoted by Samuel Bacharach, "Thomas Edison Was Right: 'Vision Without Execution Is Hallucination'," Inc., August 16, 2018. https://www.inc.com/samuel-bacharach/what-is-leadership-really-about.html.

14. Michael Dell and James Kaplan, *Play Nice but Win: A CEO's Journey from Founder to Leader* (New York: Portfolio/Penguin, 2021).

15. Herb Kelleher, quoted in Kevin Freiberg and Jackie Freiberg, *Nuts! Southwest Airlines' Crazy Recipe for Business and Personal Success* (New York: Broadway Books, 1996).

16. CBS News. "Hermès and the Success of the Coveted Birkin Bag | 60 Minutes." YouTube video, March 24, 2025.

17. Visual Capitalist, "Ranked: Most Popular AI Tools by Monthly Site Visits," March 24, 2025.

18. "Full Keynote: Satya Nadella at Microsoft Ignite 2023," YouTube video, 1:27:46, posted by Microsoft, November 15, 2023.

19. Fast Company. "The World's Most Innovative Companies of 2025," March 18, 2025. https://www.fastcompany.com/most-innovative-companies/list.

20. OpenAI, "Nubank Elevates Customer Experiences with OpenAI," March 7, 2025. https://openai.com/index/nubank/.

21. Michelle Vaccaro, Abdullah Almaatouq, and Thomas Malone, "When Combinations of Humans and AI Are Useful: A Systematic Review and Meta-Analysis," *Nature Human Behaviour* 8, no. 10 (October 28, 2024): 2293–2303, https://doi.org/10.1038/s41562-024-02024-1.

22. Kunal Handa et al., "Which Economic Tasks Are Performed with AI? Evidence from Millions of Claude Conversations," Anthropic, February 2025.

Chapter 6: Adaptability

1. David Rock, *Your Brain at Work: Strategies for Overcoming Distraction, Regaining Focus, and Working Smarter All Day Long* (New York: Harper Business, 2009).

2. Julian De Freitas et al., "Self-Orienting in Human and Machine Learning," *Nature Human Behaviour* 7, no. 12 (December 2023): 2126–2139, https://doi.org/10.1038/s41562-023-01696-5.

3. Clayton M. Christensen, *The Innovator's Dilemma: When New Technologies Cause Great Firms to Fail* (New York: HarperBusiness, 2011).
4. Karthik Valmeekam, Kaya Stechly, and Subbarao Kambhampati, "LLMs Still Can't Plan; Can LRMs? A Preliminary Evaluation of OpenAI's o1 on PlanBench," arXiv preprint, last modified September 20, 2024.
5. Prudential Financial, Inc., "Prudential, Vitality Global Expand Partnership in Latin America," news release, February 28, 2023.
6. Brock Bastian, "Why We Need Pain to Feel Happiness," TEDxStKilda, March 2017.

Chapter 7: Antifragility

1. NBA, "There Is No Failure In Sports—Giannis Addresses Comments on 'Failure' Postgame Conference," YouTube video, April 27, 2023.
2. Friedrich Nietzsche, *Twilight of the Idols*, trans. Duncan Large (Oxford: Oxford University Press, 1998), 33.
3. Nassim Nicholas Taleb, *Antifragile: Things That Gain from Disorder* (New York: Random House, 2012).
4. Amy C. Edmondson, *Right Kind of Wrong: The Science of Failing Well* (New York: Atria Books, 2023).
5. Steve Gorman and Arlene Eiras, "SpaceX Rocket Explosion Illustrates Elon Musk's 'Successful Failure' Formula," *Reuters*, April 20, 2023.
6. Yian Yin, Yang Wang, James A. Evans, and Dashun Wang, "Quantifying the Dynamics of Failure Across Science, Startups, and Security," *Nature* 575, no. 7781 (October 30, 2019): 190–194, https://doi.org/10.1038/s41586-019-1725-y.

Chapter 8: Empathy

1. *Her*. Directed by Spike Jonze. Burbank, CA: Warner Bros. Pictures, 2013. IMDb. https://www.imdb.com/title/tt1798709/.
2. Businessolver, *2024 State of Workplace Empathy: Empathy Under Pressure, Part 1* (West Des Moines, IA: Businessolver, 2024). https://businessolver.com/workplace-empathy/.
3. Cognizant Center for the Future of Work, *The Purpose Gap*, January 2022. https://www.cognizant.com/en_us/insights/documents/the-purpose-gap-codex7086.pdf.

4. Shep Hyken, *2024 Customer Service and CX Research*. https://hyken .com/research/.

5. Jacob Israelashvili et al., "Emotion Recognition from Realistic Dynamic Emotional Expressions Cohere with Established Emotion Recognition Tests: A Proof-of-Concept Validation of the Emotional Accuracy Test," *Journal of Intelligence* 9, no. 2 (2021): 25, https://doi.org/10.3390/ jintelligence9020025.

6. *Selena Gomez: My Mind & Me*. Directed by Alek Keshishian. Apple TV+, 2022. https://tv.apple.com/us/movie/selena-gomez-my-mind--me/ umc.cmc.7n5rz5krvnfcw5r6jcldxfig7.

7. Rosalind W. Picard, *Affective Computing* (Cambridge, MA: MIT Press, 1997).

8. Zohar Elyoseph et al., "Capacity of Generative AI to Interpret Human Emotions from Visual and Textual Data: Pilot Evaluation Study," *JMIR Human Factors* 11, no. 1 (2024): e50914.

9. Kashmir Hill, "She Is in Love with ChatGPT," *New York Times*, January 15, 2025.

10. Tarik Endale et al., "Barriers and Drivers to Capacity-Building in Global Mental Health Projects," *International Journal of Mental Health Systems* 14 (2020), 89, https://pubmed.ncbi.nlm.nih.gov/33292389/.

11. Hailey Fowler and John Lester, "How AI Could Expand and Improve Access to Mental Healthcare," *Oliver Wyman*, November 1, 2024. https://www.oliverwyman.com/our-expertise/perspectives/health/2024/ november/how-ai-could-expand-and-improve-access-to-mental-healthcare.html.

12. Teddy Rosenbluth, "This Therapist Helped Clients Feel Better. It Was A.I.," *New York Times*, April 15, 2025.

13. Yidan Yin, Nan Jia, and Cheryl J. Wakslak, "AI Can Help People Feel Heard, but an AI Label Diminishes This Impact," *Proceedings of the National Academy of Sciences of the United States of America* 121, no. 14 (April 2, 2024): e2319112121.

14. Hervey M. Cleckley, *The Mask of Sanity: An Attempt to Clarify Some Issues About the So-Called Psychopathic Personality*, 5th ed. (Augusta, GA: Emily S. Cleckley, 1988).

15. Dr. Kristine Gloria, "Artificial Intimacy," *The Aspen Institute Roundtable on Artificial Intelligence*. The Aspen Institute, 2020. https://www.aspen institute.org/publications/artificial-intimacy/.

Chapter 9: Trust

1. PwC, *Trust in US Business Survey*, March 12, 2024. https://www.pwc.com/us/en/library/trust-in-business-survey.html.
2. Michelle Faverio and Alec Tyson, "What the Data Says About Americans' Views of Artificial Intelligence," *Pew Research Center*, November 21, 2023. https://www.pewresearch.org/short-reads/2023/11/21/what-the-data-says-about-americans-views-of-artificial-intelligence/.
3. Salesforce Staff, "77% of Workers Trust an Autonomous AI Future. Humans Are Critical to Getting There," *Salesforce Newsroom*, June 26, 2024. https://www.salesforce.com/news/stories/autonomous-ai-research/.
4. Edelman, *2024 Edelman Trust Barometer: Key Insights Around AI*, March 2024. https://www.edelman.com/trust/2024/trust-barometer.
5. California Department of Insurance, *Bulletin 2022-5: Allegations of Racial Bias and Unfair Discrimination in Marketing, Rating, Underwriting, and Claims Practices by the Insurance Industry*, June 30, 2022.
6. EU Artificial Intelligence Act, *EU Artificial Intelligence Act*, artificialintelligenceact.eu, accessed June 5, 2025.
7. Liz Grennan et al., "Why Businesses Need Explainable AI—and How to Deliver It," *McKinsey & Company*, September 29, 2022.
8. Ying Bao et al., "Investigating the Relationship Between AI and Trust in Human–AI Collaboration," in *Proceedings of the 54th Hawaii International Conference on System Sciences*, 2021, 607–616.
9. Kambiz Saffarizadeh, Mark Keil, and Likoebe Maruping, "Relationship Between Trust in the AI Creator and Trust in AI Systems: The Crucial Role of AI Alignment and Steerability," *Journal of Management Information Systems* 41, no. 3 (2024): 645–681.

Chapter 10: Agency

1. Claudio Novelli, Mariarosaria Taddeo, and Luciano Floridi, "Accountability in Artificial Intelligence: What It Is and How It Works," *AI & Society* 39, no. 4 (2024): 1871–1882.
2. Kara Swisher, "A Wise Man Leaves Facebook," *New York Times*, September 27, 2018.
3. Benjamin Lipscomb, "Philippa Foot," *Stanford Encyclopedia of Philosophy*, edited by Edward N. Zalta, Fall 2021 Edition.
4. Moral Machine, moralmachine.net, accessed June 5, 2025.
5. Bloomberg Originals, "What Happens When Robots Don't Need Us Anymore?," YouTube video, November 16, 2024.

6. Antonio Chella, "Artificial Consciousness: The Missing Ingredient for Ethical AI?," *Frontiers in Robotics and AI* 10 (November 21, 2023). https://doi.org/10.3389/frobt.2023.1270460.

7. Reid Hoffman and Greg Beato, *Superagency: What Could Possibly Go Right with Our AI Future* (New York: Simon & Schuster, 2025).

Conclusion

1. Sebastian Krakowski, Johannes Luger, and Sebastian Raisch, "Artificial Intelligence and the Changing Sources of Competitive Advantage," *Strategic Management Journal* 43, no. 2 (February 2022): 4198–4217.

2. Daisuke Wakabayashi and Jin Yu Young, "Defeated by A.I., a Legend in the Board Game Go Warns: Get Ready for What's Next," *New York Times*, July 10, 2024.

Acknowledgments

I have to be honest: writing this book has been one of the most intellectually rewarding—and emotionally demanding—journeys of my life. And it would never have come to life without the support, inspiration, and guidance of so many incredible people along the way.

First and foremost, my sincere thanks to the entire Wiley team for believing in this project and handling every step of the process with such professionalism. A special shout-out to Leah Zarra and Gabriela Mancuso—thank you for your trust, your energy, and your exceptional partnership. You are amazing.

To my brilliant development editor, Angela Morrison—thank you for helping me make sense of my (often chaotic) ideas and shaping them into something coherent and powerful. Your clarity, patience, and insight made all the difference.

To my lifelong agent, Diego Travez—thank you for recognizing something in me nearly a decade ago and for walking with me through every step of this journey in the world of professional speaking. And to my incredible team—Rodrigo Lima, Virginia Freitas, and Alexander Souza—I love working with you, and I'm grateful every day for your talent and loyalty.

To all the 257 respondents to the "AI's Impact on Human Skills in the Workplace" survey my company conducted for this book, thank you for taking some time off your agenda to contribute with important insights.

To my family—thank you for keeping me grounded and reminding me who I am. To my friends—thank you for your generosity in listening to early drafts, questioning my logic, and letting me test ideas aloud. And to Erika—your unwavering love and belief in me, especially during moments of doubt, is what carried me through: this book wouldn't exist without you.

Finally, this book is dedicated to everyone who chooses curiosity over certainty, and humanity over hype—in an world increasingly dominated by Artificial Intelligence.

About the Author

ANDREA IORIO IS a leading keynote speaker on Artificial Intelligence, Digital Transformation, Leadership, and Customer-Centricity, and he shares insights at the intersection of business, technology, philosophy, and neuroscience in over 100 keynotes each year for Fortune 500 companies globally.

With more than a decade of experience in multinational and tech companies, Andrea served as Head of Tinder across Latin America for five years and later as Chief Digital Officer at L'Oréal Brazil. He holds a degree in Economics from Bocconi University (Milan) and a Master's in International Relations from Johns Hopkins University's SAIS (Washington, DC). He currently teaches in the MBA program at Fundação Dom Cabral.

He is a columnist for MIT Technology Review Brasil and WIRED Mexico, host of NVIDIA's official podcast in Brazil, and has a social media following of over 100,000 people.

Based in Miami with his family, Andrea is also a black belt in Brazilian Jiu-Jitsu.

Index